GRAND TOUR OF ITALY

- - - - - - - - - - - - - - - - - -

ROAD TRIPS

This edition written and researched by

**Cristian Bonetto, Duncan Garwood, Paula Hardy,
Donna Wheeler and Nicola Williams**

HOW TO USE THIS BOOK

Reviews

In the Destinations section:

All reviews are ordered in our authors' preference, starting with their most preferred option. Additionally:

Sights are arranged in the geographic order that we suggest you visit them and, within this order, by author preference.

Eating and Sleeping reviews are ordered by price range (budget, midrange, top end) and, within these ranges, by author preference.

Symbols In This Book

✅	Top Tips	🍷	Food & Drink
🔗	Link Your Trips	🌳	Outdoors
💡	Tips from Locals	📷	Essential Photo
🚗	Trip Detour	🚶	Walking Tour
📖	History & Culture	🍴	Eating
👪	Family	🛏	Sleeping

Map Legend

Routes
- Trip Route
- Trip Detour
- Linked Trip
- Walk Route
- Tollway
- Freeway
- Primary
- Secondary
- Tertiary
- Lane
- Unsealed Road
- Plaza/Mall
- Steps
- Tunnel
- Pedestrian Overpass
- Walk Track/Path

Boundaries
- International
- State/Province
- Cliff

Hydrography
- River/Creek
- Intermittent River
- Swamp/Mangrove
- Canal
- Water
- Dry/Salt/ Intermittent Lake
- Glacier

Highway Markers
- A6 Autostrada
- SS231 State Highway
- SR203 Regional Highway
- SP3 Provincial Highway
- E74 Other Road

Trips
- 1 Trip Numbers
- 9 Trip Stop
- 🔲 Walking tour
- 🔲 Trip Detour

Population
- ✪ Capital (National)
- ◉ Capital (State/Province)
- ● City/Large Town
- ● Town/Village

Areas
- Beach
- Cemetery (Christian)
- Cemetery (Other)
- Park
- Forest
- Reservation
- Urban Area
- Sportsground

Transport
- ✈ Airport
- Cable Car/ Funicular
- Ⓜ Metro station
- Ⓟ Parking
- Train/Railway
- Tram

Note: Not all symbols displayed above appear on the maps in this book

◉	Sights	🛏	Sleeping
🏖	Beaches	🍴	Eating
🏃	Activities	🍷	Drinking
🎓	Courses	☆	Entertainment
👉	Tours	🛍	Shopping
🎆	Festivals & Events	ℹ	Information & Transport

These symbols and abbreviations give vital information for each listing:

- 📞 Telephone number
- 🕐 Opening hours
- 🅿 Parking
- ⊖ Nonsmoking
- ❄ Air-conditioning
- @ Internet access
- 📶 Wi-fi access
- 🏊 Swimming pool
- 🥗 Vegetarian selection
- 📖 English-language menu
- 👪 Family-friendly

- 🐾 Pet-friendly
- 🚌 Bus
- ⛴ Ferry
- 🚊 Tram
- 🚆 Train
- apt apartments
- d double rooms
- dm dorm beds
- q quad rooms
- r rooms
- s single rooms
- ste suites
- tr triple rooms
- tw twin rooms

CONTENTS

CONTENTS

ROAD TRIPS

DESTINATIONS

ROAD TRIP ESSENTIALS

View over Piazzo San Pietro, Rome (p56)
ALBERTO SO / EYEEM / GETTY IMAGES ©

Palazzo Carignano (p91), Turin

WELCOME TO
THE GRAND TOUR OF ITALY

Italy, the *bel paese* (beautiful country), is one of Europe's great seducers.

Blessed with an unparalleled cultural heritage, food that is imitated the world over and a landscape that combines historic cities, stunning coastlines and remote wildernesses, Italy has been beguiling travellers for centuries, and still casts a powerful spell today.

Follow the trail of bohemians and intellectuals as you wind your way between the country's star cities, enjoying a wealth of lesser-known historic treasures and artistic masterpieces along the way.

GRAND TOUR OF ITALY

1 Grand Tour
The classic cultural tour – part pilgrimage, part rite of passage. **12–14 DAYS**

3 Piero della Francesca Trail
A Renaissance art tour through medieval towns and dramatic mountain passes. **7 DAYS**

4 **Italian Riviera**
Cruise through a perennially stylish collection of coastal towns.
4 DAYS

2 **Roaming Around Rome**
Rome's hinterland is littered with little-known historic sites.
3 DAYS

Isole
Tremiti

PUGLIA

Foggia

MOLISE

Campobasso

Benevento

Isernia

Avellino

CAMPANIA

Chieti

Monte Amaro
(2795m)

Caserta

Mt Vesuvius
(1281m)

Salerno

Naples

Golfo di
Napoli

Golfo di
Salerno

Capri

Parco Nazionale
del Cilento e
Vallo di Diano

Parco Nazionale
del Gran Sasso e
Monti della Laga

Corno Grande
(2912m)

L'Aquila

ABRUZZO

Frosinone

Golfo di
Gaeta

Ischia

Golfo di
Policastro

Aeolian
Islands

UMBRIA

Rieti

Latina

Capo
Circeo

Tevere

Terni

LAZIO

Monte Cavo
(949m)

ROME ★

Lago di
Bracciano

Viterbo

Lago di
Bolsena

Monte Amiata
(1736m)

Lago di
Bolsena

Civitavecchia

Grosseto

Giglio

Montecristo

Pianosa

Tyrrhenian
Sea

Corsica

FRANCE

Ajaccio

Olbia

Sassari

Nuoro

Parco Nazionale
del Golfo di Orosei
e del Gennargentu

Oristano

Punta
La Marmora
(1834m)

SARDINIA

Cagliari

San
Pietro

Sant'Antioco

0   200 km
0   100 miles

GRAND TOUR OF ITALY
HIGHLIGHTS

★

Alassio (above) This elegant beach town has been a favourite holiday spot for European expats for almost 300 years. See it on Trip **4**

Ostia Antica (left) While Rome abounds with historic sites (and tourists), many miss one of Italy's most compelling and under-appreciated archaeological treasures. See it on Trip **2**

Sansepolcro (right) Birthplace of Piero della Francesca, this charming town abounds in historic *palazzi* and great works of art. See it on Trip **3**

CITY GUIDE

ROME

Even in a country of exquisite cities, Rome (Roma) is special. Pulsating, seductive and utterly disarming, it's a mesmerising mix of artistic masterpieces and iconic monuments, theatrical piazzas and haunting ruins. If your road leads to Rome, give yourself a couple of days to explore its headline sights.

St Peter's Basilica (p57)

Getting Around

Driving is not the best way to get around Rome. Traffic can be chaotic and much of the *centro storico* (historic centre) is closed to nonauthorised traffic on weekdays and weekend evenings. You're better off using public transport; a day pass is €6.

Parking

On-street parking, which is expensive and scarce, is denoted by blue lines. There are some car parks in the centre, which charge about €15 to €20 per day. Some top-end hotels offer parking, usually for an extra charge.

Discover the Taste of Rome

For authentic nose-to-tail Roman cooking check out the trattorias in Testaccio, and for traditional Roman-Jewish cuisine head to the atmospheric Jewish Ghetto.

Live Like a Local

The most atmospheric, and expensive, place to stay is the *centro storico*, where you'll have everything on your doorstep. Night owls will enjoy Trastevere, while Tridente offers refined accommodation and designer shopping. The Vatican is also popular.

Useful Websites

060608 (www.060608.it) Official tourist website.

Lonely Planet (www.lonelyplanet.com/rome) Destination low-down, hotels and traveller forum.

Trips through Rome: 1 2

Destination coverage: p56

For more, check out our city and country guides. www.lonelyplanet.com

RILINDH / GETTY IMAGES ©

TOP EXPERIENCES

➡ Get to the Heart of the Ancient City

Thrill to the sight of the Colosseum, Roman Forum and Palatino, where Romulus and Remus supposedly founded the city in 753 BC.

➡ Gaze Heavenwards in the Sistine Chapel

File past kilometres of priceless art at the Vatican Museums to arrive at the Sistine Chapel and Michelangelo's fabled frescoes. (www.vatican.va)

➡ Visit Villa Borghese's Baroque Treasures

Head to the Museo e Galleria Borghese to marvel at a series of exhilarating sculptures by baroque maestro Gian Lorenzo Bernini. (www.galleriaborghese.it)

➡ Admire the Pantheon's Dome

The Pantheon is the best preserved of Rome's ancient monuments; it's only when you get inside that you get the full measure of the place as its dome soars above you.

➡ Pay Homage at St Peter's Basilica

Capped by Michelangelo's landmark dome, the Vatican's showpiece church is a masterpiece of Renaissance architecture and baroque decor.

➡ Live the Trastevere Dolce Vita

Join the evening crowds in Trastevere to eat earthy Roman food, drink in the many bars and pubs, and parade up and down the streets.

➡ Hang Out on the Piazzas

Hanging out on Rome's piazzas is part and parcel of Roman life – having an ice cream on Piazza Navona, people-watching on Piazza del Popolo and posing on Piazza di Spagna.

Via de'Tornabuoni, Florence (p66)

FLORENCE

An essential stop on every Italian itinerary, Florence (Firenze) is one of the world's great art cities, boasting Renaissance icons and a wonderfully intact *centro storico*. Beyond the Michelangelo masterpieces and Medici *palazzi* (mansions), there's a buzzing bar scene and great shopping in artisan workshops and designer boutiques.

Getting Around

Nonresident traffic is banned from the centre of Florence for most of the week, and if you enter the Limited Traffic Zone (ZTL) you risk a €150 fine. Rather than drive, walk or use the city buses; tickets cost €1.20 or €2 on board.

Parking

There is free street parking around Piazzale Michelangelo (park within the blue lines). Pricey (around €20 per day) underground parking can be found around Fortezza da Basso and in the Oltrarno beneath Piazzale di Porta Romana. Otherwise, ask if your hotel can arrange parking.

Discover the Taste of Florence

Florence teems with restaurants, trattorias, *osterie* (casual taverns) and wine bars catering to all budgets. Top neighbourhoods include Santa Croce, home to some of the city's best restaurants, and over-the-river Oltrarno.

Live Like a Local

To be right in the heart of it, go for the Duomo and Piazza della Signoria areas, which have some excellent budget options. Near the train station, Santa Maria Novella has some good midrange boutique/design hotels.

Useful Websites

Firenze Turismo (www.firenzeturismo.it) Official tourist office site; comprehensive and up to date.

The Florentine (www.theflorentine.com) For accommodation, sights information and practical advice.

Firenze Musei (www.firenzemusei.it) Book tickets for the Uffizi and Accademia.

Trips through Florence: 1 3

Destination coverage: p66

Grand Canal and Basilica di Santa Maria della Salute (p81)

VENICE

A magnificent, unforgettable spectacle, Venice (Venezia) is a hauntingly beautiful city. For 1000 years it was one of Europe's great sea powers and its unique cityscape reflects this, with golden Byzantine domes and great Gothic churches, noble *palazzi* and busy waterways.

Getting Around

Venice is off-limits to cars, leaving you to walk or take a boat. You'll inevitably get lost at some point but directions to Piazza San Marco, the Rialto and Accademia are posted on yellow signs. *Vaporetti* (small ferries) ply the city's waterways; a one-way ticket costs €7.

Parking

Once you've crossed the Ponte della Libertà bridge from Mestre, you'll have to park at Piazzale Roma or Tronchetto car parks; bank on up to €26 for 24 hours.

Discover the Taste of Venice

Venice's version of tapas, bar snacks called *cicheti,* are served in *osterie* across town at lunch and between 6pm and 8pm.

Live Like a Local

Many Venetians open their historic homes as B&Bs – check the Turismo Venezia website for lists. Dorsoduro and San Polo are charming areas to stay in, near major museums and with plenty of bar action. Cannaregio is another good option, relatively untouristy and in parts very picturesque.

Useful Websites

Turismo Venezia (www. turismovenezia.it) The city's official tourism site.

A Guest in Venice (www. unospitedivenezia.it) Hotelier association that provides information on upcoming exhibits, events and lectures.

Veneto Inside (www. venetoinside.com) Book entry to the Basilica di San Marco, guided visits and water taxis.

Trips through Venice:

Destination coverage: p77

NEED ^{TO} KNOW

CURRENCY
Euro (€)

LANGUAGE
Italian

VISAS
Generally not required for stays of up to 90 days (or at all for EU nationals); some nationalities need a Schengen visa (p128).

FUEL
You'll find filling stations on autostradas and all major roads. The price of fuel can be higher in Italy than in neighbouring countries; be sure to check before you go.

RENTAL CARS
Avis (www.avis.com)

Europcar (www.europcar.com)

Hertz (www.hertz.com)

Maggiore (www.maggiore.it)

IMPORTANT NUMBERS
Ambulance (☎118)

Emergency (☎112)

Police (☎113)

Roadside Assistance (☎803 116; ☎800 116800 from a foreign mobile phone)

Climate

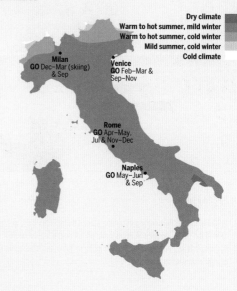

Dry climate
Warm to hot summer, mild winter
Warm to hot summer, cold winter
Mild summer, cold winter
Cold climate

Milan
GO Dec–Mar (skiing) & Sep

Venice
GO Feb–Mar & Sep–Nov

Rome
GO Apr–May, Jul & Nov–Dec

Naples
GO May–Jun & Sep

When to Go

High Season (Jul–Aug)
» Prices high on the coast; accommodation discounts available in some cities in August.

» Prices rocket for Christmas, New Year and Easter.

» Late December to March is high season in the Alps and Dolomites.

Shoulder Season (Apr–Jun & Sep–Oct)
» Good deals on accommodation, especially in the south.

» Spring is best for festivals, flowers and local produce.

» Autumn provides warm weather and the grape harvest.

Low Season (Nov–Mar)
» Prices at their lowest – up to 30% less than in high season.

» Many sights and hotels closed in coastal and mountainous areas.

» A good period for cultural events in large cities.

Daily Costs

Budget: Less than €100

» Double room in a budget hotel: €50–€100

» Pizza or pasta: €6–€12

» Excellent markets and delis for self-catering

Midrange: €100–€200

» Double room in a midrange hotel: €80–€180

» Lunch and dinner in local restaurants: €25–€45

» Museum admission: €5–€15

Top End: More than €200

» Double room in a four- or five-star hotel: €200–€450

» Top-restaurant dinner: €50–€150

» Opera tickets: €15–€150

Eating

Restaurants (Ristoranti) Formal service and refined dishes, with prices to match.

Trattorias Family-run places with informal service and classic regional cooking.

Vegetarians Most places offer good vegetable starters and side dishes.

Price indicators for a meal with *primo* (first course), *secondo* (second course), a glass of house wine and *coperto* (cover charge):

€	less than €25
€€	€25–€45
€€€	more than €45

Sleeping

Hotels From luxury boutique palaces to modest family-run *pensioni* (small hotels).

B&Bs Rooms in restored farmhouses, city *palazzi* (mansions) or seaside bungalows.

Agriturismi Farmstays range from working farms to luxury rural retreats.

Price indicators for a double room with bathroom and breakfast included:

€	less than €110
€€	€110–€200
€€€	more than €200

Arriving in Italy

Leonardo da Vinci (Fiumicino) Airport (Rome)

Rental cars Agencies are near the multilevel car park. Look for signs in the Arrivals area.

Trains & buses Run every 30 minutes from 6.30am to 11.40pm.

Night buses Hourly departures from 12.30am to 5am.

Taxis Set fare €48; 45 minutes.

Malpensa Airport (Milan)

Rental cars In Terminal 1 agencies are on the 1st floor; in Terminal 2 in the Arrivals hall.

Malpensa Express & Shuttle Runs every 30 minutes from 5am to 11pm.

Night buses Limited services from 12.15am to 5am.

Taxis Set fare €90; 50 minutes.

Capodichino Airport (Naples)

Rental cars Agencies are located in the main Arrivals hall.

Airport shuttles Run every 20 minutes from 6.30am to 11.40pm.

Taxis Set fare €19 to €23; 30 minutes.

Mobile Phones (Cell Phones)

Local SIM cards can be used in European, Australian and unlocked, multiband US phones. Other phones must be set to roaming.

Internet Access

Wifi is available in many lodgings and city bars, often free. Internet cafes are thin on the ground and typically charge €2 to €6 per hour.

Money

ATMs at airports, most train stations and in towns and cities. Credit cards accepted in most hotels and restaurants. Keep cash for immediate expenses.

Tipping

Not obligatory but round up the bill in pizzerias and trattorias; 10% is normal in upmarket restaurants.

Useful Websites

Italia (www.italia.it) Official tourism site.

Michelin (www.viamichelin.it) A useful route planner.

Agriturismi (www.agriturismi. it) Guide to farmstays.

Lonely Planet (www. lonelyplanet.com/italy) Destination low-down.

For more, see Road Trip Essentials (p115).

Road Trips

San Remo (p51)
JULIUS FEKETE / SHUTTERSTOCK ©

Grand Tour

The gap-year journey of its day, the Grand Tour is a search for art and enlightenment, adventure and debauchery.

TRIP HIGHLIGHTS

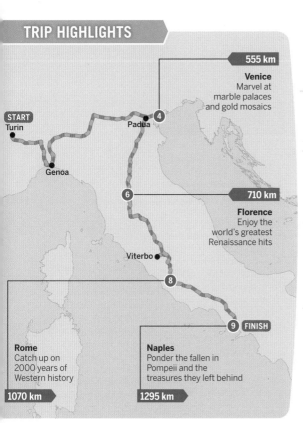

555 km

Venice
Marvel at marble palaces and gold mosaics

START
Turin

Padua

Genoa

710 km

Florence
Enjoy the world's greatest Renaissance hits

Viterbo

FINISH

Rome
Catch up on 2000 years of Western history

1070 km

Naples
Ponder the fallen in Pompeii and the treasures they left behind

1295 km

12–14 DAYS
1295KM / 804 MILES

GREAT FOR...

BEST TIME TO GO
Spring (March–May) is perfect for urban sightseeing.

 ESSENTIAL PHOTO

Florence's multicoloured, marble Duomo (Cathedral).

BEST FOR HISTORY

Rome, the repository of over 2500 years of European history.

ft Duomo (p26), Florence

1 Grand Tour

From the Savoy palaces of Turin and Leonardo's *Last Supper* to the dubious drinking dens of Genoa and the pleasure palaces of Rome, the Grand Tour is part scholar's pilgrimage and part rite of passage. Offering a chance to view some of the world's greatest masterpieces and hear Vivaldi played on 18th-century cellos, it is a rollicking trip filled with the sights, sounds and tastes that have shaped European society for centuries.

❶ Turin (p90)

In his travel guide, *Voyage through Italy* (1670), travel writer and tutor Richard Lassels advocated a grand cultural tour of Europe, and in particular Italy, for young English aristocrats, during which the study of classical antiquity and the High Renaissance would ready them for future influential roles shaping the political, economic and social realities of the day.

First they travelled through France before crossing the Alps at Mt Cenis and heading to Turin (Torino), where letters of introduction admitted them to the city's agreeable Parisian-style social whirl. Today Turin's tree-lined boulevards retain their elegant, French feel and many turn-of-the century cafes, such as **Caffè San Carlo** (Piazza San Carlo 156; ⊘8am-1am), still serve Torinese hot chocolate beneath their gilded chandeliers.

Like the Medicis in Florence (Firenze) and the Borghese in Rome (Roma), Turin's Savoy princes had a penchant for extravagant architecture and interior decor. You suspect they also pined for their hunting lodges in Chambéry, France, from where they originated,

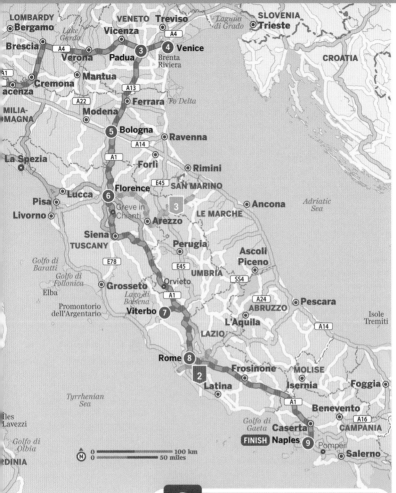

as they invited André le Nôtre, Versailles landscaper, to design the gardens of **Palazzo Reale** (Piazza Castello; adult/reduced €12/6; 8.30am-7.30pm Tue-Sun) in 1697.

The Drive » The two-hour (170km) drive to Genoa is all on the autostrada, the final stretch twisting through the mountains. Leave Turin following signs for

LINK YOUR TRIP

2 Roaming Around Rome

If the Eternal City becomes too exhausting, escape to some lesser-known sights in the Roman hinterland (p31).

3 Piero della Francesca Trail

From Florence, jump on to this art-based trail and take in masterpieces, medieval towns and striking scenery (p39).

the A55 (towards Alessandria), which quickly merges with the A21 passing through the pretty Piedmontese countryside. Just before Alessandria turn south onto the A26 for Genoa/Livorno.

❷ Genoa (p98)

Some travellers, shy of crossing the Alps, might arrive by boat in Genoa (Genova). Despite its superb location, mild microclimate and lush flora, the city had a dubious reputation. Its historic centre was a warren of dark, insalubrious *caruggi* (alleys), stalked by prostitutes and beggars, while the excessive shrewdness of the Genovese banking families earned them a reputation, according to author Thomas Nugent, as 'a treacherous and over-reaching set of people'.

And yet with tourists and businesspeople arriving from around the world, Genoa was, and still is, a cosmopolitan place. The Rolli Palaces, a collection of grand mansions originally meant to host visiting popes, dignitaries and royalty, made Via Balbi and Strada Nuova (now Via Giuseppe Garibaldi) two of the most famous streets in Europe. Visit the finest of them, the **Palazzo Spinola** (Galleria Nazionale; www.palazzospinola. beniculturali.it; Piazza Superiore di Pellicceria 1; adult/ reduced €4/2; ⊗8.30am-8pm Tue-Sat, from 1.30pm Sun) and the **Palazzo Reale** (www.palazzorealegenova. beniculturali.it; Via Balbi 10; adult/child €4/2; ⊗9am-7pm Thu-Sun, to 1.30pm Tue & Wed). Afterwards stop for sweets at **Pietro Romanengo fu Stefano** (www.romanengo.com; Via Soziglia 74r).

The Drive » This 365km drive takes most of the day, so stop for lunch in Cremona. Although the drive is on the autostrada, endless fields of corn line the route. Take the A7 north out of Genoa and at Tortona exit onto the A21 around industrial Piacenza to Brescia. At Brescia, change again onto the A4 direct to Padua.

❸ Padua (p86)

Bound for Venice (Venezia), Grand Tourists could hardly avoid visiting Padua (Padova), although by the 18th century international students no longer flocked to **Palazzo del Bò** (☎049 827 30 47; Via VIII Febbraio; adult/reduced €5/2; ⊗tours 9.15am, 10.15am & 11.15pm Tue, Thu & Sat, 3.15pm, 4.15pm & 5.15pm Mon, Wed & Fri), the Venetian Republic's radical university where Copernicus and Galileo taught class.

You can visit the university's claustrophobic, wooden anatomy theatre (the first in the world),

DETOUR: MILAN

Start: ❶ Turin

No Grand Tour would be complete without a detour up the A4 to Milan (Milano) to eyeball Leonardo da Vinci's iconic **Il Cenacolo** (The Last Supper; www. cenacolovinciano.net; Piazza Santa Maria delle Grazie 2; adult/ reduced €6.50/3.25; ⊗8.15am-7pm Mon-Sat). Advance booking is essential (booking fee €1.50).

From his *Portrait of a Young Man* (c 1486), to portraits of Duke Ludovico Sforza's beautiful mistresses, *The Lady with the Ermine* (c 1489) and *La Belle Ferronière* (c 1490), da Vinci transformed the rigid conventions of portraiture to depict highly individual images imbued with naturalism. Then he evolved concepts of idealised proportions and the depiction of internal emotional states through physical dynamism *(St Jerome)*, all of which cohere in the masterly *Il Cenacolo*.

although it's no longer *de rigueur* to witness dissections on the average tourist itinerary. Afterwards don't forget to pay your respects to the skulls of noble professors who donated themselves for dissection because of the difficulty involved in acquiring fresh corpses. Their skulls are lined up in the graduation hall.

Beyond the university the melancholy air of the city did little to detain foreign visitors. Even Giotto's spectacular frescoes in the **Scrovegni Chapel** (www.cappelladegliscrovegni. it; Piazza Eremitani 8; adult/ reduced €13/6; night ticket €8/6; ⏰9am-7pm), where advance reservations are essential, were of limited interest given medieval art was out of fashion, and only devout Catholics ventured to revere the strange relics of St Anthony in the **Basilica di Sant'Antonio** (www.basilicadelsanto.org; Piazza del Santo; ⏰6.30am-7.45pm, to 6.45pm Nov-Mar).

The Drive ≫ Barely 50km, the drive from Padua to Venice is through featureless areas of light industry along the A4 and then the A57.

– – – – – – – – – –

TRIP HIGHLIGHT

❹ Venice (p77)

Top of the itinerary, Venice at last! Then, as now, *La Serenissima's* watery landscape captured the imagination of travellers. At **Carnevale** (www.carnevale.venezia.it) in February numbers swelled to 30,000; now they number in the hundreds of thousands. You cannot take your car onto the lagoon islands so leave it in a secure garage in Mestre, such as **Garage Europa** (www.garageeuropamestre. com; per day €14), and hop on the train to Venice Santa Lucia where water taxis connect to all the islands.

Aside from the mind-improving art in the **Gallerie dell'Accademia** (www.gallerieaccademia. org; Campo della Carità 1050; adult/reduced €11/8; plus exhibition supplement; ⏰8.15am-2pm Mon, to 7.15pm Tue-Sun), extraordinary architectural follies such as the **Palazzo Ducale**, the **Campanile** and Longhena's **Basilica di Santa Maria della Salute**, and the glittering Eastern domes of **Basilica di San Marco** (www. basilicasanmarco.it; Piazza San Marco; basilica entry free; ⏰9.45am-5pm Mon-Sat, 2-5pm Sun), Venice was considered, according to author Bruce Redford, the 'locus of decadent Italianate allure'. Venetian wives were notorious for keeping handsome escorts (*cicisbeo*), courtesans held powerful positions at court and much time was devoted to frequenting casinos and coffeehouses. Historic **Caffè Florian** (www. caffeflorian.com; Piazza San Marco 56/59; drinks €10-25; ⏰9am-midnight) still adheres to rules established in the 1700s.

So do as the Venetians would do, glide down the **Grand Canal** on the **No 1 vaporetto** (small passenger ferry; ticket €6.50) for an architectural tour of 50 *palazzi* (mansions), gossip in the balconies of the **Teatro La Fenice** (☎reservations 041 24 24; www.teatrolafenice.it; Campo San Fantin 1965; theatre visits adult/reduced €9/6), or listen for summer thunderstorms in Vivaldi's *Four Seasons*, played by **Interpreti Veneziani** (www. interpretiveneziani.com; Chiesa San Vidal; adult/reduced €27/22; ⏰8.30pm).

For more earthly pleasures visit the produce-piled **Campo Rialto Mercato** (San Polo, Campo de la Pescaria, ⏰7am-2pm Mon-Sat) and the covered seafood market, **Pescaria** (Rialto, ⏰7am-2pm Tue-Sun).

The Drive ≫ Retrace your steps to Padua on the A57 and A4 and navigate around the ring road in the direction of Bologna to pick up the A13 southwest for this short 1½-hour drive. After Padua the dual carriageway dashes through wide-open farmland and crosses the Po river which forms the southern border of the Veneto.

⑤ Bologna

Home to Europe's oldest university (established in 1088) and once the stamping ground of Dante, Boccaccio and Petrarch, Bologna had an enviable reputation for courtesy and culture. Its historic centre, complete with 20 soaring towers, is one of the best-preserved and largest medieval cities in the world.

In its **Basilica di San Petronio** (Piazza Maggiore; admission free; ⊙7.45am-2pm & 3-6.30pm), originally intended to dwarf St Peter's in Rome, Giovanni Cassini's sundial (1655) proved the problems with the Julian calendar, giving us the leap year, while Bolognesi students advanced human knowledge in obstetrics, natural science, zoology and anthropology. You can peer at their strange model waxworks and studiously labelled collections in the **Palazzo Poggi** (www.museopalazzopoggi.unibo.it; Via Zamboni 33; adult/reduced €5/3; ⊙10am-4pm Tue-Fri, 10.30am-5.30pm Sat & Sun; shorter hrs winter).

Leading in art as in science, the School of Bologna gave birth to the Carracci cousins Ludovico, Agostino and Annibale, who were among the founding fathers of Italian baroque and were

Top left Statue, Piazza Maggiore, Bologna
Far left Pompeii (p28)
Left Venice (p23)

25

deeply influenced by the Counter-Reformation. See their emotionally charged blockbusters in the **Pinacoteca Nazionale** (Via delle Belle Arti 56; admission €4; ☺9am-7pm Tue-Sun).

The Drive » Bologna sits at the intersection of the A1, A13 and A14. From the centre navigate west out of the city, across the river Reno, onto the A1. From here it's a straight shot into Florence for 110km, leaving the Po plains behind you and entering the low hills of Emilia-Romagna and the forested valleys of Tuscany.

❻ Florence (p66)

From Filippo Brunelleschi's red-tiled dome atop Florence's **Duomo** (www.operaduomo. firenze.it; Piazza del Duomo; admission €10; ☺10am-5pm Mon-Wed & Fri, to 4.30pm Thu, to 4.45pm Sat, 1.30-4.45pm Sun) to Michelangelo's and Botticelli's greatest hits, *David* and *The Birth of Venus* respectively,

in the **Galleria dell'Accademia** (☎055 294 883; Via Ricasoli 60; adult/reduced €8/4; ☺8.15am-6.50pm Tue-Sun) and the **Galleria degli Uffizi** (www.uffizi.firenze.it; Piazza degli Uffizi 6; adult/reduced €8/4; ☺8.15am-6.50pm Tue-Sun), Florence, according to Unesco, contains 'the greatest concentration of universally renowned works of art in the world'.

Whereas Rome and Milan have torn themselves down and been rebuilt many times, incorporating a multitude of architectural whims, central Florence looks much as it did in 1550, with stone towers and cypress-lined gardens.

The Drive » The next 210km, continuing south along the A1, travels through some of Italy's most lovely scenery. Just southwest of Florence the vineyards of Greve in Chianti harbour some great farmstays, while Arezzo is to the east. At Orvieto exit onto the SS71 and skirt Lago di Bolsena for the final 50km into Viterbo.

TOP TIP: JUMP THE QUEUE IN FLORENCE

In July, August and other busy periods such as Easter, long queues are a fact of life at Florence's key museums. For a fee of €4 each, tickets to the Uffizi and Galleria dell'Accademia (where *David* lives) can be booked in advance. To organise your ticket, go to www.firenzemusei.it or call **Firenze Musei** (Florence Museums; ☎055 29 48 83; ☺booking line 8.30am-6.30pm Mon-Fri, to 12.30pm Sat), which also has **ticketing desks** (☺8.30am-7pm Tue-Sun) at the Uffizi and Palazzo Pitti.

❼ Viterbo

From Florence the road to Rome crossed the dreaded and pestilential *campagna* (countryside), a swampy, mosquito-infested low-lying area. Unlike now, inns en route were uncomfortable and hazardous, so travellers hurried through Siena stocking up on wine for the rough road ahead. They also stopped briefly in medieval Viterbo for a quick douse in the thermal springs at the **Terme dei Papi** (☎07 61 35 01; www.termedeipapi.it; Strada Bagni 12; pool €12, Sun €25; ☺9am-7pm Wed-Mon, plus 9.30pm-1am Sat), and a tour of the High Renaissance spectacle that is the **Villa Lante** (☎07 6128 8008; admission €2; ☺8.30am-1hr before sunset Tue-Sun).

The Drive » Rejoin the A1 after a 28km drive along the rural SS675. For the next 40km the A1 descends slowly into Lazio, criss-crossing the river Tevere and keeping the ridge of the Apennines to the left as it darts through tunnels. At Fiano Romano exit for Roma Nord onto the A1dir for the final 20km descent into the capital.

❽ Rome (p56)

In the 18th century Rome, even in ruins, was still thought of as the august capital of the world. Here more than anywhere the Grand Tourist was awakened to an interest in art and architecture,

Colosseum

although the **Colosseum** (Piazza del Colosseo; www.coopculture.it; adult/reduced incl Roman Forum & Palatino €12/7.50; ☺8.30am-1hr before sunset) was still filled with debris and the Palatino was covered in gardens, its excavated treasures slowly accumulating in the world's oldest national museum, the **Capitoline Museums** (Musei Capitolini; www.museicapitolini.org; Piazza del Campidoglio 1; adult/reduced €11.50/9.50; ☺9.30am-7.30pm, last admission 6.30pm;).

Arriving through the Porta del Popolo, visitors first espied the dome of **St Peter's** (Piazza San Pietro; audioguides €5; ☺7am-7pm) before clattering along the *corso* to the customs house. Once done, they headed to **Piazza di Spagna**, the city's principal meeting place, where Keats penned his love poems and died of consumption.

Although the **Pantheon** (Piazza della Rotonda; admission free; ☺8.30am-7.30pm Mon-Sat, 9am-6pm Sun) and **Vatican Museums** (http://mv.vatican.va; Viale Vaticano; adult/reduced €16/8; ☺9am-4pm Mon-Sat, 9am-12.30pm last Sun of month) were a must, most travellers

preferred to socialise in the grounds of the **Borghese Palace** (www.galleriaborghese.it; Piazzale del Museo Borghese 5; adult/reduced €11/6.50; ☺9am-7pm Tue-Sun, prebooking necessary).

Follow their example and mix the choicest sights with more venal pleasures such as fine dining at **Open Colonna** (☎06 4782 2641; Via Milano 9a; meals €20-80; ☺12.30-midnight Tue-Sat, lunch Sun) and souvenir shopping at antique perfumery **Officina Profumo Farmaceutica di Santa Maria Novella** (Corso Rinascimento 47).

TOP TIP: ROME INFORMATION LINE

The Comune di Roma (city council) runs a free multilingual **information line** (☎06 06 08; www.060608.it; ⊕9am-9pm), providing information on culture, shows, hotels, transport etc. You can also book theatre, concert, exhibition and museum tickets on this number. The call centre, open 24 hours, has staff who speak English, French, Arabic, German, Spanish, Italian and Chinese available from 4pm to 7pm.

The Drive » Past Rome the landscape is hotter and drier, trees give way to Mediterranean shrubbery and the grass starts to yellow. Beyond the vineyards of Frascati, just 20km south of Rome, the A1 heads straight to Naples (Napoli) for 225km, a two-hour drive that often takes much longer due to heavy traffic.

TRIP HIGHLIGHT

❾ Naples (p104)

Only the more adventurous Grand Tourists continued south to the salacious southern city of Naples.

At the time **Vesuvius** (www.epnv.it; crater tours €8; ⊕9am-6pm Jul & Aug, to 5pm Apr-Jun & Sep, to 4pm Mar & Oct, to 3pm Nov-Feb) glowed menacingly on the bay, erupting no less than six times during the 18th century and eight times in the 19th century. But Naples was the home of opera and *commedia dell'arte* (improvised comedic drama satirising stock social stereotypes), and singing lessons and seats at **Teatro San Carlo** (☎box office 081 797 23 31,

guided tours 081 553 45 65; www.teatrosancarlo.it; Via San Carlo 98; tours €6; ⊕10am-4.30pm Mon-Sat, prebooking necessary) were obligatory.

Then there were the myths of Virgil and Dante to explore at Lago d'Averno and **Campi Flegrei** (the Phlegrean Fields). And, after the discovery of **Pompeii** (☎081 857 53 47; www.pompeiisites.org; entrances at Porta Marina, Piazza Esedra & Piazza Anfiteatro; adult/reduced €11/5.50; ⊕8.30am-7.30pm summer, to 5pm winter) in 1748, the unfolding drama of a Roman town in its death throes drew throngs of mawkish voyeurs. Then, as now, it was the most popular tourist sight in Italy and its priceless mosaics, pornographic frescoes and colossal sculptures filled the **Museo Archeologico Nazionale** (☎081 442 21 49; Piazza Museo Nazionale 19; admission adult/reduced €8/4; ⊕9am-7.30pm Wed-Mon).

Piazza di Spagna & the Spanish Steps (p27), Rome

THOMAS STANKIEWICZ / LOOK-FOTO / GETTY IMAGES ©

Roaming Around Rome

2

Rome's little-explored hinterland is a real eye-opener, with verdant scenery and thrilling cultural treasures – haunting ancient ruins, hilltop villas and landscaped Renaissance gardens.

TRIP HIGHLIGHTS

97 km

Villa Adriana
Explore the remnants of Hadrian's lavish country residence

101 km

Tivoli
Fountains, frescoes and landscaped Renaissance gardens

5 **6** FINISH

● Palestrina

3

Grottaferrata ●

● Marino

● Castel Gandolfo

45 km

Frascati
Food, wine, great views and ancient artefacts

1 START

Ostia Antica
The beautifully preserved ruins of ancient Rome's seaport

0 km

3 DAYS
101KM / 62 MILES

GREAT FOR...

BEST TIME TO GO

Spring's good for the ancient sites, early summer for romantic views.

 ESSENTIAL PHOTO

Fountains at Tivoli's Villa d'Este.

 BEST FOR WINE BUFFS

Frascati's traditional cellars.

2 Roaming Around Rome

While Rome (Roma) hogs the limelight, the area around the capital makes for an absorbing drive with its wealth of historic sights. Headline acts include the remarkably well-preserved ruins of ancient Rome's port at Ostia Antica, and Emperor Hadrian's vast palace complex at Tivoli. Tivoli is one of several hilltop towns that feature on this trip, along with the wine town of Frascati and the papal retreat of Castel Gandolfo.

TRIP HIGHLIGHT

① Ostia Antica

The remarkably well-preserved ruins of Ostia Antica, ancient Rome's main seaport, form one of Italy's most compelling and underappreciated archaeological sites. The city was founded in the 4th century BC at the mouth of the Tiber and developed into a major port with a population of around 100,000. Decline came in the 5th century when barbarian invasions and

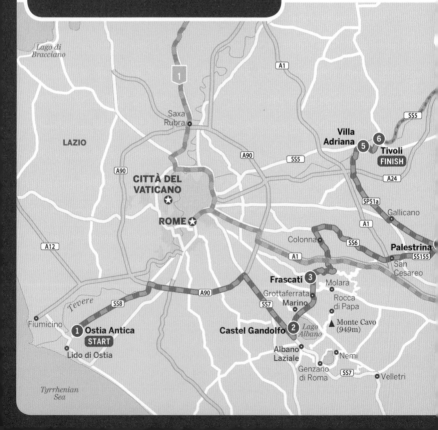

an outbreak of malaria led to its abandonment and slow burial in river silt, thanks to which it has survived so well.

The **Scavi Archeologici di Ostia Antica** (Ruins of Ostia Antica; www.ostiaantica.beniculturali.it; Viale dei Romagnoli 717; adult/reduced €10/6; ☺8.30am-6.15pm Tue-Sun summer, earlier closing winter) are spread out and you'll need a few hours to do them justice. The main thoroughfare, the **Decumanus Maximus**, leads from the city's entrance (the Porta Romana) to highlights such as the **Terme di Nettuno** (Baths of Neptune), whose floor features a famous mosaic of Neptune driving his seahorse chariot. Next door, the steeply stacked **amphitheatre** was built by Agrippa and later enlarged to hold 3000 people. Behind the theatre, the **Piazzale delle Corporazioni** (Forum of the Corporations) housed Ostia's merchant guilds and is decorated with well-preserved mosaics. Further towards Porta Marina, the **Thermopolium** is an ancient cafe complete with a bar and fresco advertising the bill of fare.

The Drive » Head back towards Rome and take the Grande Raccordo Anulare (GRA) for Naples. Exit at the Ciampino Airport turn-off and continue up Via Appia (SS7), until you come to traffic lights halfway up a long climb. Make a left turn to Lago Albano and follow this road up under the towering umbrella pines to Castel Gandolfo at the top. All told, it takes about 35 minutes.

ABRUZZO

A24

p36

Subiaco

A1

1

Segni

0 ——— 10 km
0 ——— 5 miles

🅢 LINK YOUR TRIP

1 Grand Tour
Use this trip to extend the classic Grand Tour of Italy, which sweeps from Naples through Rome and on to Florence and Venice (p19).

② Castel Gandolfo

One of the prettiest towns in the Castelli Romani, an area of wooded wine-rich hills just south of Rome, Castel Gandolfo makes for a memorable stop. It's not a big place but what it lacks in size it makes up for in atmosphere, and on a warm summer's evening there's no better place for a romantic tête-à-tête. Action is centred on **Piazza della Libertà**, a refined baroque square overlooked by the **Palazzo Pontificio** (closed to visitors), the pope's impressive summer residence. But a stop here is not so much about sightseeing as lapping up the gorgeous views over Lago Albano and enjoying a leisurely al fresco meal.

The Drive » To Frascati it's a pretty straightforward 20-minute drive. From Castel Gandolfo follow the road for Marino, enjoying glimpses of the lake off to your right, and then Grottaferrata. Here you'll come to a roundabout. Take the third exit and Frascati is 4km further on.

TRIP HIGHLIGHT

③ Frascati

Best known for its crisp white wine, Frascati is a popular day-trip destination. On hot summer weekends Romans pile into town to hang out in the elegant historic centre and fill up on *porchetta* (herb-roasted pork) and local wine. You can follow suit by filling up from the food stalls on **Piazza del Mercato** or searching out the traditional *cantinas* (originally wine and olive-oil cellars, now informal restaurants) that pepper the centre's narrow lanes. Once you've explored the town and admired the sweeping views from the tree-lined avenue at the bottom of Piazza Marconi, head up to **Villa Aldobrandini**. Designed by Giacomo della Porta and built by Carlo Maderno, this regal 16th-century villa sits haughtily above town in a stunning hillside position. The villa itself is closed to the public but you can visit the impressive early baroque **gardens** (Via Cardinal Massai 18; admission free; ⊙ dawn-dusk) dramatically landscaped into the wooded hill.

PAVEL068 / GETTY IMAGESS ©

The Drive ⟩⟩ Take Viale Catone from the top of Piazza Marconi, following the green signs for the autostrada. Continue, passing through Colonna, until soon afterwards you hit the fast-flowing SS6 (Via Casilina). Turn right onto the Casilina and after San Cesareo, left onto the SS155 for a twisting climb up to Palestrina. Plan on about half an hour from Frascati.

- - - - - - - - - - - -

❹ Palestrina

The pretty town of Palestrina stands on the slopes of Monte Ginestro, one of the foothills of the Apennines. In ancient times Praeneste, as it was then known, was a favourite summer retreat for wealthy Romans and the site of a much-revered temple dedicated to the goddess of fortune. Little remains intact of the 2nd-century-BC **Santuario della Fortuna Primigenia**, but much of what is now the historic centre was built over its six giant terraces.

Nowadays, the town's main act is the fantastic **Museo Archeologico Nazionale di Palestrina** (Piazza della Cortina; admission €5; ⊙ 9am-8pm), housed in the 17th-century **Palazzo Colonna Barberini**. Highlights of the museum's collection include the wonderful 'Capitoline Triad', a marble sculpture of Jupiter, Juno and Minerva; and a

Gardens of Villa Aldobrandini

spectacular 2nd-century-BC mosaic showing the flooding of the Nile, an incredibly rich depiction of daily life in ancient Egypt.

The Drive » It takes just over half an hour to get to Villa Adriana. Exit Palestrina and head northwest towards Gallicano. Here, follow the signs to Tivoli, continuing past the shrubbery and under the Castello di Passerano until you see Villa Adriana signposted a few kilometres short of Tivoli.

TRIP HIGHLIGHT

⑤ Villa Adriana

Emperor Hadrian's sprawling 1st-century summer residence, **Villa Adriana** (☎0774 38 27 33; adult/reduced €8/4; ☉9am-1hr before sunset) was one of ancient Rome's grandest properties, designed to be lavish even by the decadent standards of the day. Hadrian

personally designed much of the complex, taking inspiration from buildings he'd seen around the world. The pecile, a large porticoed pool, was a reproduction of a building in Athens, and the canopo is a copy of the sanctuary of Serapis near Alexandria – its long canal of water was originally surrounded by Egyptian statues, representing the Nile.

To the east of the pecile is Hadrian's private retreat, the **Teatro Marittimo**. Built on an island in an artificial pool, it was originally a mini-villa accessible only by 'bascule bridges', which the emperor would have raised when he felt like a dip. There are also a nymphae, temples and barracks, and a museum (often closed) which contains the latest discoveries from ongoing excavations.

The Drive » Pick up Via Tiburtina (SS5), the main Rome–Tivoli road, and head up to Tivoli centro. It's a short, steep, twisting climb up to the town centre, which should take about 15 minutes.

TRIP HIGHLIGHT

⑥ Tivoli

Tivoli's elevated historic centre is an attractive, if often busy, spot. Its main attraction is the Unesco-protected **Villa d'Este** (www.villadestetivoli.info; Piazza Trento; adult/reduced €8/4; ⏰8.30am-1hr before sunset Tue-Sun), a one-time Benedictine convent

that Lucrezia Borgia's son, Cardinal Ippolito d'Este, transformed into a pleasure palace in 1550. From 1865 to 1886 it was home to Franz Liszt and inspired his compositions *To the Cypresses of the Villa d'Este* and *The Fountains of the Villa d'Este*.

The villa's rich mannerist frescoes merit a glance, but it's the garden that you're here for: water-spouting gargoyles and elaborate avenues lined with deep-green, knotty cypresses and extravagant fountains. Highlights include the **Fountain of the Organ**, an extravagant baroque ensemble that uses water pressure to play music through a concealed organ, and the 130m-long **Avenue of the Hundred Fountains**, which joins the Fountain of Tivoli to the Fountain of Rome.

DETOUR: SUBIACO

Start: ⑥ **Tivoli**

Remote-feeling and dramatic, Subiaco is well worth the trip to see its two breathtaking Benedictine monasteries. The **Monastery of St Benedict** (admission free; ⏰9am-12.15pm & 3.30-6.15pm) is carved into the rock over the cave where St Benedict holed up for three years to meditate and pray. Apart from its stunning setting, described by Petrarch as 'the edge of Paradise', it's adorned with rich 13th- to 15th-century frescoes.

Halfway down the hill from St Benedict is the **Monastery of St Scholastica** (⏰9.30am-12.15pm & 3.30-6.15pm), the only one of the 13 monasteries built by St Benedict still standing in the Valley of the Aniene. If you decide to stay, its **Foresteria** (📞07 748 55 69; www.benedettini-subiaco.org; per person B&B €58) is a great place to spend a contemplative night. But book ahead, as Benedictine clergy from around the world often make the pilgrimage here to work in the monastery's famous library and archive. There's also a restaurant offering set menus for €19 and €27.

Neptune Fountain, Villa d'Este

ALESSANDRO0770 / GETTY IMAGES ©

Piero della Francesca Trail

3

Follow in the footsteps of the Renaissance painter Piero della Francesca as you wind your way from the medieval centre of Urbino to Florence, stopping en route to admire his greatest works.

TRIP HIGHLIGHTS

0 km

Urbino
A charming Renaissance hill town surrounded by green peaks

72 km

Sansepolcro
Piero della Francesca's birthplace, a real hidden gem

FINISH
6

Passo della Consuma

Poppi

1
START

3

Passo di Bocca Trabaria (1049m)

5

Monterchi

90 km

Arezzo
Revel in sublime frescoes in the art-rich historic centre

Florence
Home to the world's greatest collection of Renaissance art

172 km

7 DAYS
172KM / 107 MILES

GREAT FOR...

BEST TIME TO GO
June to September for summer pageantry.

ESSENTIAL PHOTO

Views from the Passo della Consuma.

BEST FOR FILM BUFFS

Arezzo's Piazza Grande, a location for scenes in *La vita è bella*.

Piero della Francesca Trail

The Piero della Francesca trail was first advocated by the British author Aldous Huxley in *The Best Picture*, a 1925 essay he wrote in praise of della Francesca's *Resurrezione* (Resurrection). The roads have improved since Huxley's day but the trail remains a labour of love for art fans as it leads through dramatic Apennine scenery, over mountain passes and on to bustling medieval towns, culminating in Italy's revered Renaissance city, Florence (Firenze).

TRIP HIGHLIGHT

① Urbino

Hidden away in hilly Le Marche, the charming town of Urbino was a key player in the Renaissance art world. Its ruler, the Duca Federico da Montefeltro, was a major patron and many of the top artists and intellectuals of the day spent time here at his behest. Piero della Francesca arrived in 1469 and, along with a crack team of artists

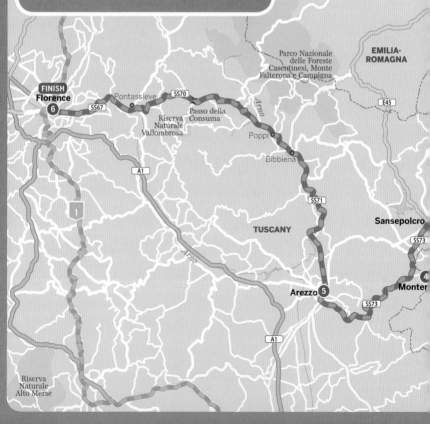

and architects, worked on the duke's palatial residence, the **Palazzo Ducale** (☎199 151123; www. palazzoducaleurbino.it; Piazza Duca Federico; adult/reduced €12/9.50; ☺8.30am-2pm Mon, to 7.15pm Tue-Sun). This magnificent palace now houses the **Galleria Nazionale delle Marche** and its rich collection of Renaissance paintings, including Piero della Francesca's great *Flagellazione di Cristo* (Flagellation of Christ).

A short walk away, you can pay homage to Urbino's greatest son at the **Casa Natale di Raffaello** (Via Raffaello 57; adult/reduced €3.50/2.50; ☺9am-7pm Mon-Sat, 10am-1pm & 3-6pm Sun), the house where superstar painter Raphael was born in 1483.

The Drive ›› The 50km (1½-hour) drive up to the Passo di Bocca Trabaria involves hundreds of hairpin bends and tortuous climbing as it traverses a magnificent swathe of Apennine mountains. From Urbino pick up the SS73bis and head through Montesoffio and Urbania before climbing up to the pass.

❷ Passo di Bocca Trabaria

The Bocca Trabaria mountain pass (1049m) divides the Valtiberina (Tiber Valley), on the Urbino side, from the upper Valle del Metauro (Metauro Valley). It's a spectacular spot, well worth a quick pause, with sweeping views over the Apennines and several hiking trails heading into the surrounding mountains.

The Drive ›› Allow about half an hour for the 20km descent from Bocca Trabaria to Sansepolcro. For the first 15km or so the winding road plunges down the valley slopes to San Giustino, from where it's an easy hop northwest to Sansepolcro on the SS3bis.

TRIP HIGHLIGHT

❸ Sansepolcro

Birthplace of Piero della Francesca and home to three of his great works, Sansepolcro is an authentic hidden gem. Its unspoiled historic centre

LINK YOUR TRIP

Grand Tour
Turn this trip into a detour from Florence as you follow in the footsteps of 18th-century intellectuals travelling from Turin to Naples (p19).

EMILIA-ROMAGNA

❶ Urbino **START**

Montesoffio

SS73bis

Urbania

SS73bis

LE MARCHE

Metauro

❷ Passo di Bocca Trabaria

...istino

UMBRIA

Parco Regionale del Monte Cucco

Tevere

E45

Ⓝ 0 ____ 20 km
0 ____ 10 miles

41

is littered with *palazzi* (mansions) and churches harbouring great works of art, including the 14th-century **Cattedrale di San Giovanni Evangelista** (Via Giacomo Matteotti 4; ⊘10am-noon & 4-7pm), which contains an *Ascension* by Perugino. The highlight, though, is the **Museo Civico** (www.museocivicosansepolcro.it; Via Aggiunti 65; adult/reduced €8/5; ⊘10am-1.30pm & 2.30-7pm, shorter hrs winter), whose small but top-notch collection boasts three Piero della Francesca masterpieces: *Resurrezione* (Resurrection; c 1460), the *Madonna della Misericordia* (c 1455–60) and *Saint Julian* (1455–58).

The Drive ⟩⟩ Head southwest from Sansepolcro along the SS73 following signs for Arezzo. After roughly 12km of easy driving through pleasant countryside, turn left onto the SP221 and continue for 3km to Monterchi. It takes about 25 minutes.

- - - - - - - - - - - -

④ Monterchi

This unassuming village boasts one of Piero della Francesca's best-loved works, the *Madonna del Parto* (Pregnant Madonna, c 1460). Housed in its own museum, the **Museo della Madonna del Parto** (Via della Reglia 1; adult/reduced €6.50/5; ⊘9am-1pm & 2-5pm Wed-Mon), it depicts a heavily pregnant Madonna wearing a

simple blue gown and standing in a tent, flanked by two angels who hold back the tent's curtains as a framing device. In a nice touch, pregnant women get free entry to the museum.

The Drive ⟩⟩ Double back the way you came and turn left onto the quick-running SS73. The road, which opens to four lanes in certain tracts, snakes its way through thickly wooded hills up to Arezzo.

- - - - - - - - - - - -

TRIP HIGHLIGHT

⑤ Arezzo

The biggest town in eastern Tuscany, Arezzo

has a distinguished cultural history. Petrarch and art historian Giorgio Vasari were both born here, and, between 1452 and 1466, Piero della Francesca painted one of his greatest works, the *Leggenda della Vera Croce* (Legend of the True Cross) fresco cycle in the **Basilica di San Francesco's Cappella Bacci** (Piazza San Francesco; adult/reduced €8/5; ⊘9am-6.30pm Mon-Fri, 9am-5.30pm Sat, 1pm-5.30pm Sun).

Once you've seen that, take time to admire the magnificent Romanesque facade of the **Pieve di**

Della Francesca's *Flagellazione di Cristo* (p41), Urbino

Santa Maria (Corso Italia 7; ⊙8am-12.30pm & 3-6.30pm) en route to the **Cattedrale di San Donato** (Piazza Duomo; ⊙7am-12.30pm & 3-6.30pm) and yet another della Francesca fresco – the exquisite *Mary Magdalene* (c 1460).

Film buffs should also stop by **Piazza Grande**, where scenes were filmed for Roberto Benigni's *La vita è bella* (Life is Beautiful), and where the city celebrates its big annual festival, the **Joust of the Saracino**, on the third Saturday in June and first Sunday in September.

The Drive ≫ The quickest route to Florence is via the A1 autostrada, but you'll enjoy the scenery more if you follow the SS71 up the Casentino valley and on to the medieval castle town of Poppi. At Poppi pick up the SS70 to tackle the heavily forested Passo della Consuma (1050m) and descend to Pontassieve and the SS67 into Florence. Allow about 2¾ hours.

PIERO DELLA FRANCESCA

Though many details about his life are hazy, it's believed that Piero della Francesca was born around 1420 in Sansepolcro and died in 1492. Trained as a painter from 15, his distinctive use of perspective, mastery of light and skilful synthesis of form and colour set him apart from his artistic contemporaries. His most famous works are the *Leggenda della Vera Croce* (Legend of the True Cross) in Arezzo, and *Resurrezione* (Resurrection) in Sansepolcro, but he is most fondly remembered for his luminous *Madonna del Parto* (Pregnant Madonna) in Monterchi.

THE RENAISSANCE

Bridging the gap between the Middle Ages and the modern world, the Renaissance (*il Rinascimento*) emerged in 14th-century Florence and quickly spread throughout Italy.

The Early Days

Giotto di Bondone (1267–1337) is generally considered the first great Renaissance artist, and with his exploration of perspective and a new interest in realistic portraiture, he inspired artists such as Lorenzo Ghiberti (1378–1455) and Donatello (c 1382–1466). In architectural terms, the key man was Filippo Brunelleschi (1377–1446), whose dome on Florence's Duomo was one of the era's blockbuster achievements. Of the following generation, Sandro Botticelli (c 1444–1510) was a major player and his *Birth of Venus* (c 1485) was one of the most successful attempts to resolve the great conundrum of the age – how to give a painting both a realistic perspective and a harmonious composition.

The High Renaissance

By the early 16th century, the focus had shifted to Rome and Venice. Leading the way in Rome was Donato Bramante (1444–1514), whose classical architectural style greatly influenced the Veneto-born Andrea Palladio (1508–80). One of Bramante's great rivals was Michelangelo Buonarotti (1475–1564), whose legendary genius was behind the Sistine Chapel frescoes, the dome over St Peter's Basilica, and the *David* sculpture. Other headline acts included Leonardo da Vinci (1452–1519), who developed a painting technique (sfumato) enabling him to modulate his contours using colour; and Raphael (1483–1520), who more than any other painter mastered the art of depicting large groups of people in a realistic and harmonious way.

---

❻ Florence

The last port of call is Florence, the city where the Renaissance kicked off in the late 14th century. Paying the way was the Medici family, who sponsored the great artists of the day and whose collection today graces the **Galleria degli Uffizi** (Uffizi Gallery; www.uffizi.firenze.it; Piazza degli Uffizi 6; adult/reduced €8/4, incl temporary exhibition €12.50/6.25; ⏰8.15am-6.50pm Tue-Sun). Here you can admire Piero della Francesca's famous portrait of the red-robed *Duke and Duchess of Urbino* (1465–1472) alongside works by Renaissance giants, from Giotto and Cimabue to Botticelli, Leonardo da Vinci, Raphael and Titian.

Elsewhere in town, you'll find spiritually uplifting works by Fra' Angelico in the wonderful **Museo di San Marco** (Piazza San Marco 1; adult/reduced €4/2; ⏰8.15am-1.50pm Mon-Fri, to 4.50pm Sat & Sun, closed 1st, 3rd, 5th Sun & 2nd & 4th Mon of month), and superb frescoes by Masaccio, Masolino da Panicale and Filippino Lippi at the **Cappella Brancacci** (☎055 276 82 24; Piazza del Carmine 14; admission adult/reduced €6/4.50; ⏰10am-5pm Wed-Sat & Mon, 1-5pm Sun, booking necessary), over the river in the Basilica di Santa Maria del Carmine.

Cappella Brancacci

PHOTOGOLFER / SHUTTERSTOCK ©

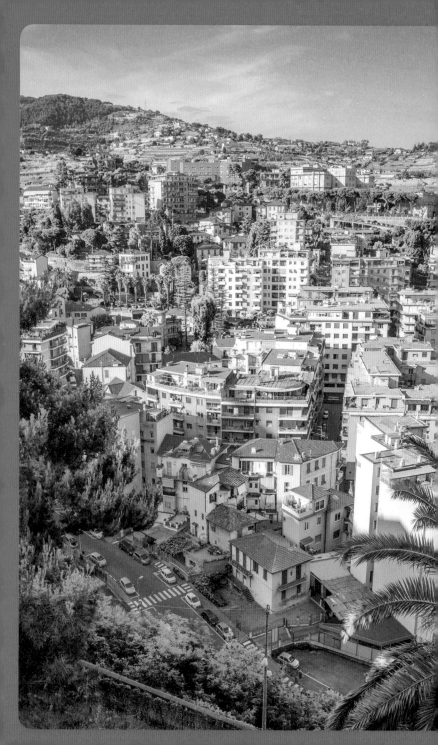

Italian Riviera

4

Curving west in a broad arc, backed by the Maritime Alps, the Italian Riviera sweeps down from Genoa through ancient hamlets and terraced olive groves to the French border at Ventimiglia.

TRIP HIGHLIGHTS

107 km

Alassio
The preferred holiday spot of presidents and artists

0 km

Genoa
For big-city grit and glamour

1
START

Savona

3

4

Taggia

6

Andora

Ventimiglia
FINISH

San Remo
Italy's wannabe Monte Carlo

165 km

Finale Ligure
Provides a sandy shore nestled between two rivers

74 km

4 DAYS
182KM / 113 MILES

GREAT FOR...

BEST TIME TO GO
April, May and June for flowers and hiking; October for harvest.

ESSENTIAL PHOTO
Cascading terraces of exotic flowers at Giardini Botanici Hanbury.

BEST FINE DINING
Purple San Remo prawns on the terrace of San Giorgio.

San Remo (p51)

4 Italian Riviera

The contrast between sun-washed, sophisticated coastal towns and a deeply rural, mountainous hinterland, full of heritage farms, olive oil producers and wineries, gave rise to the Riviera's 19th-century fame, when European expatriates outnumbered locals. They amused themselves in lavish botanical gardens, gambled in the casino of San Remo and dined in style in fine art-nouveau villas, much as you will on this tour.

TRIP HIGHLIGHT

❶ Genoa (p98)

Like Dr Jekyll and Mr Hyde, Genoa (Genova) is a city with a split personality. At its centre, medieval *caruggi* (alleys) untangle outwards to the **Porto Antico** and teem with hawkers, merchants and office workers. Along Via Garibaldi and Via XXV Aprile is another Genoa, one of Unesco-sponsored palaces, smart shops and grand architectural gestures like **Piazza de Ferrari**

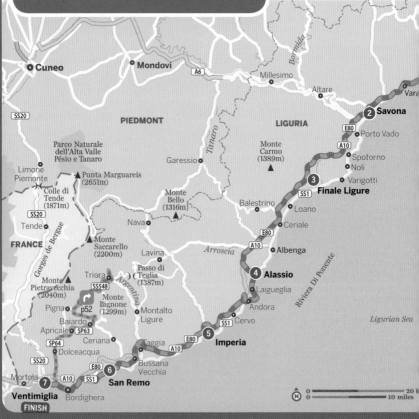

with its monumental fountain, art nouveau **Palazzo Borsa** (once the city's stock exchange) and the neoclassical **Teatro Carlo Felice** (www.carlofelice.it; Passo Eugenio Montale 4).

Join the well-dressed *haute bourgeoisie* enjoying high-profile art exhibits in the grand Mannerist halls of the **Palazzo Ducale** (www.palazzoducale.genova.it; Piazza Giacomo Matteotti 9; admission €5-10; ⏰ exhibitions 9am-9pm Tue-Sun), then retire to sip *spritz* amid Bernardino Strozzi's 17th-century

frescoes at **Cambi Cafe** (www.cambicafe.com; Vico Falamonica 9; ⏰10am-11pm).

The Drive » Exit Genoa westward, through a tangle of flyovers and tunnels to access the A10 for the first 48km drive to Savona. Once out of the suburbs the forested slopes of the Maritime Alps rise to your right and sea views peep out at you as you duck through tunnels.

- - - - - - - - - - - -

② Savona

Don't be put off by Savona's horrifying industrial sprawl; the Savonesi were a powerful maritime people and the town centre is unexpectedly graceful. Standing near the port are three of the many medieval towers that once studded the cityscape. Genoa's greatest rival, the town was savagely sacked in 1528, the castle dismantled and most of the population slaughtered, but somehow the **Fortezza del Priamàr** (Piazza Priamar) and the **Cattedrale di**

LINK YOUR TRIP

Grand Tour
Arrive at Genoa by following the trail of bohemians and intellectuals from Naples through Rome and on to Italy's north (p19).

Nostra Signora Assunta (Piazza Cattedrale) survived.

But you're not here for the architecture – you're here for the food. The covered **market** (Via Pietro Giuria; ⏰7am-1.30pm Mon-Sat) is crammed with fruit-and-veg stalls and fish stands stacked with salt cod. **Grigiomar** (Via P Giuria 5-2; ⏰Tue-Sun) salts its own local anchovies. Then there are the local *amaretti* biscuits, made with bitter and sweet almonds, available at **Pasticceria Besio** (www.amarettibesio.com; Via Sormano 16r; ⏰Tue-Sat), and the *farinata di grano* (wheat-flour pancakes) at **Vino e Farinata** (Via Pia 15; ⏰11am-10pm Tue-Sat).

The Drive » Rejoin the A10 and leave the industrial chimneys of Savona behind you. For the first 13km the A10 continues with views of the sea, then at Spotorno it ducks inland for the final 15km to the Finale Ligure exit. Descend steeply for 3km to the Finale hamlets on the coast.

- - - - - - - - - - - -

TRIP HIGHLIGHT

③ Finale Ligure

Finale Ligure comprises several seaside districts. The marina is narrow and charming, spreading along the sandy shore between two small rivers, the Porra and the Sciusa. East of the Sciusa is Finale Ligure Pia, where you'll find **Alimentari Magnone** (Via Moletti 17), which stocks excellent extra virgin olive oils from local growers. Nearby the Benedictine abbey houses the **Azienda Agricola Apiario Benedettino** (Via al Santuario 59; ⊘Mon-Sat), where you can buy honey, grappa and organic beauty products.

At the other end of town, **Finalborgo** is the old medieval centre. Each year in March, Finalborgo's cloisters are home to the **Salone dell'Agroalimentare Ligure**, where local farmers hawk seasonal delicacies and vintages.

On Thursday it's worth driving 9km up the coast to picturesque **Noli** for the weekly outdoor market on Corso d'Italia.

The Drive ⟫ Once again take the high road away from the coast and follow the A10 for a further 35km to Alassio. At Albenga you'll cross the river Centa and the broad valley where dozens of hothouses dot the landscape.

- - - - - - - - - -

TRIP HIGHLIGHT

❹ Alassio

Less than 100km from the French border, Alassio's popularity among the 18th- and 19th-century jet set has left it with an elegant colonial character. Its pastel-hued villas range around a broad, sandy beach, which stretches all the way to **Laigueglia** (4km to the west). American

president Thomas Jefferson holidayed here in 1787 and Edward Elgar composed *In the South* inspired by his stay in 1904. **Il Muretto**, a ceramic-covered wall, records the names of 550 celebrities who've passed through.

Follow the local lead and promenade along Via XX Settembre or the unspoiled waterfront. Take coffee at **Antico Caffè Pasticceria Balzola** (www.balzola. net; Piazza Matteotti 26; ⊘Tue-Sun Dec-Oct) and enjoy gelato on the beach beneath a stripy umbrella.

The Drive ⟫ If you have time take the scenic coast road, SS1 (Via Roma), from Alassio through Laigueglia, to Andora, before rejoining the autostrada. It adds about 5km to the journey but is a scenic jaunt when traffic is light. From Andora it's a further 16km on the A10 to Imperia.

- - - - - - - - - -

❺ Imperia

Imperia consists of two small seaside towns, Oneglia and Porto Maurizio, on either side of the Impero river.

Oneglia, birthplace of Admiral Doria, the Genoese Republic's greatest naval hero, is the less attractive of the two, although **Piazza Dante**, with its arcaded walkways, is a great place for artisanal coffee at **Caffè Piccardo** (Piazza Dante 1; ⊘6.30am-8.30pm).

ZM.PHOTO / SHUTTERSTOCK ©

This is also where the great olive-oil dynasties made their name. Visit the **Museo dell'Olio** (www.museodellolivo.com; tickets adult/reduced €5/2.50; ⊘9am-12.30pm & 3-6.30pm Mon-Sat) in the landscaped grounds of the Fratelli Carli factory, where a pair of 1000-year-old olive trees guard the entrance to 18 spot-lit caverns detailing the history of the Ligurian industry. You can buy oil here or at award-winning **Ranise** (www.ranise.it; Via Nazionale 30).

West of Oneglia is pirate haven **Porto Maurizio**, perched on a rocky spur that overlooks a yacht-filled harbour.

Pier on the Alassio seafront

The Drive » Rejoining the A10 at Imperia, the landscape begins to change. The olive terraces are dense, spear-like cypresses and umbrella pines shade the hillsides, and the fragrant *maquis* (Mediterranean scrub) is prolific. Loop inland around Taggia and then descend slowly into San Remo.

- - - - - - - - - -

TRIP HIGHLIGHT

❻ San Remo

San Remo, Italy's wannabe Monte Carlo, is a sun-dappled Mediterranean resort with a grand belle époque **casino** (www. casinosanremo.it; Corso degli Inglesi; ⊘10am-late) and lashings of Riviera-style grandeur.

During the mid-19th century the city became a magnet for European nobility such as Tsar Nicolas of Russia, who favoured the town's balmy winters. Russian devotees built an onion-domed **Russian Orthodox church** (Via Nuvoloni 2; admission €1; ⊘9.30am-noon & 3-6pm), reminiscent of Moscow's

SAN GIORGIO

Cult restaurant **San Giorgio** (☎0183 40 01 75; www. ristorantesangiorgio.com; Via A Volta 19, Cervo; ⊘lunch & dinner Wed-Mon Feb-Dec) has been quietly wowing gourmets with its authentic Ligurian cooking since the 1950s when mother-and-son team Caterina and Alessandro opened the doors of their home in the *borgo* (medieval town) of **Cervo Alta**. Dine out on the bougainvillea-draped terrace in summer, or in intimate dining rooms cluttered with family silverware and antiques in winter. Below the restaurant, in an old oil mill, is the less formal wine bar and deli **San Giorgino**.

DETOUR: L'ENTROTERRA

Start: **7** Ventimiglia

The designation 'Riviera' omits the pleated, mountainous interior – *l'entroterra* – that makes up nine-tenths of Liguria. Harried by invasions, coast-dwellers took to these vertical landscapes over a thousand years ago, hewing their perched villages from the rock face of the Maritime Alps. You'll want to set aside two extra days to drive the coiling roads that rise up from Ventimiglia to **Dolceacqua**, **Apricale** and **Pigna**. If you make it all the way to **Triora**, book into the **Colomba d'Oro** (☏0184 9 40 51; www.colombadoro.it; d €70-110; Ⓟ). It's worth it for the breakfast and the see-forever panoramas.

St Basil's Cathedral, which still turns heads down by the seafront. Swedish inventor Alfred Nobel also maintained a villa here, the **Villa Nobel** (Corso Felice Cavallotti 112; ◷10am-12.30pm Tue-Sun, 3-6pm Fri-Sun), which now houses a museum dedicated to him and his work.

Beyond the waterfront, San Remo hides a little-visited old town, a labyrinth of twisting lanes that cascades down the Ligurian hillside. Curling around the base is the **Italian**

Cycling Riviera, a path that tracks the coast as far as Imperia. For bike hire, enquire at the **tourist office** (www. visitrivieradeifiori.it; Largo Nuvoloni 1; ◷9am-7pm Mon-Sat, 9am-1pm Sun).

The Drive » For the final 17km stretch to Ventimiglia take the SS1 coastal road, which hugs the base of the mountains and offers uninterrupted sea views. In summer and Easter, however, when traffic is heavy, your best bet is the A10.

----

7 Ventimiglia

Despite its enviable position between the glitter of San Remo and the Côte d'Azur, Ventimiglia is a soulful but disorderly border town, its Roman past still evident in its bridges, amphitheatre and ruined baths. Now it's the huge **Friday market** (Piazza della Libertà; ◷8am-3pm) that draws the crowds.

If you can't find a souvenir here then consider one of the prized artisanal honeys produced by **Marco Ballestra** (www. mielepolline.it; Via Girolamo Rossi 5; ◷Tue-Sat), which has hives in the hills above the Valle Roya. There are over a dozen different types.

To end the tour head over to the pretty western suburb of Ponte San Ludovico to the **Giardini Botanici Hanbury** (www.giardini hanbury.com; Corso Montecarlo 43, La Mortola; adult/reduced €7.50/4.50; ◷9.30am-6pm), the 18-hectare estate of English businessman Sir Thomas Hanbury; he planted it with an extravagant 5800 botanical species from five continents.

Destinations

Rome (p56)
No trip through Italy would be complete without a visit to the Eternal City – a place that has dazzled visitors for centuries.

Florence (p66)
Cradle of the Renaissance and of tourist masses that flock here to feast on world-class art, Florence is magnetic, romantic and busy.

Venice & Padua (p77)
A fabled lagoon city awash with art, music and spice-route cuisine, and a medieval city-state home to Italy's second-oldest university.

Turin & Genoa (p90)
Elegant baroque Turin is only two hours from fabled port city Genoa.

Naples & Around (p104)
Naples is a love-it-or-loathe-it sprawl of operatic *palazzi* and churches, mouthwatering markets and art-crammed museums.

Piazza Grande (p43), Arezzo
FRANKVANDENBERGH / GETTY IMAGES ©

Ever since its glory days as an ancient superpower, Rome has been astonishing visitors. Its museums and basilicas showcase some of Europe's most celebrated masterpieces. But nothing can capture the sheer elation of experiencing Rome's operatic streets, baroque piazzas and colourful neighbourhood markets.

Rome

ROME

POP 2.86 MILLION

According to myth, Rome was founded on the Palatino (Palatine Hill) by Romulus, twin brother of Remus and son of Mars, god of war. Historians offer a more prosaic version of events, claiming that Romulus became the first king of Rome on 21 April 753 BC. By AD 100 Rome had a population of 1.5 million and was the undisputed *caput mundi* (capital of the world). The cityscape reflects Rome's rise and fall over the centuries, and its museums and basilicas showcase some of Europe's most celebrated masterpieces.

◉ Sights

Colosseum RUIN

(Colosseo; ☎ 06 3996 7700; www.coopculture.it; Piazza del Colosseo; adult/reduced incl Roman Forum & Palatino €12/7.50; ⊙ 8.30am-1hr before sunset; Ⓜ Colosseo) Originally known as the Flavian Amphitheatre, the 50,000-seat Colosseum is the most thrilling of Rome's ancient sights. It was here that gladiators met in combat and where condemned prisoners fought wild beasts in front of baying, bloodthirsty crowds. Visit in the early morning to avoid the crowds.

Palatino ARCHAEOLOGICAL SITE

(Palatine Hill; ☎ 06 3996 7700; www.coopculture.it; Via di San Gregorio 30 & Via Sacra; adult/reduced incl Colosseum & Roman Forum €12/7.50; ⊙ 8.30am-1hr before sunset; Ⓜ Colosseo) The Palatino is

an atmospheric area of towering pine trees, majestic ruins and memorable views. It was here that Romulus supposedly founded the city in 753 BC, and Rome's emperors lived in unabashed luxury. Look out for the **stadio** (stadium), the ruins of the **Domus Flavia** (imperial palace), and grandstand views over the Roman Forum from the **Orti Farnesiani**.

Roman Forum ARCHAEOLOGICAL SITE

(Foro Romano; ☎ 06 3996 7700; www.coopculture.it; Largo della Salara Vecchia & Via Sacra; adult/reduced incl Colosseum & Palatino €12/7.50; ⊙ 8.30am-1hr before sunset; 🚌 Via dei Fori Imperiali) An impressive – if rather confusing – sprawl of ruins, the Roman Forum was ancient Rome's showpiece centre, a grandiose district of temples, basilicas and vibrant public spaces. The site, which was originally an Etruscan burial ground, was first developed in the 7th century BC, growing over time to become the social, political and commercial hub of the Roman empire.

Beyond the basilica, the **Arco di Tito** (Arch of Titus) was built in AD 81 to celebrate Vespasian and Titus' victories against rebels in Jerusalem.

Capitoline Museums MUSEUM

(Musei Capitolini; ☎ 06 06 08; www.museicapitolini.org; Piazza del Campidoglio 1; adult/reduced €11.50/9.50; ⊙ 9.30am-7.30pm, last admission

6.30pm; 🚇 Piazza Venezia) Dating to 1471, the Capitoline Museums are the world's oldest public museums. Their collection of classical sculpture is one of Italy's finest, including crowd-pleasers such as the iconic *Lupa capitolina* (Capitoline Wolf), a sculpture of Romulus and Remus under a wolf, and the *Galata morente* (Dying Gaul), a moving depiction of a dying Gaul warrior. There's also a picture gallery with masterpieces by the likes of Titian, Tintoretto, Rubens and Caravaggio.

Pantheon   CHURCH
(Piazza della Rotonda; ⊙ 8.30am-7.30pm Mon-Sat, 9am-6pm Sun; 🚇 Largo di Torre Argentina) The Pantheon is one of Rome's most iconic sights. A striking 2000-year-old temple, now a church, it is the city's best-preserved ancient monument and one of the most architecturally influential in the Western world. The pockmarked exterior might look its age, but inside it's a different story, and it's a unique and exhilarating experience to pass through the towering bronze doors and have your vision directed upwards to the breathtaking dome.

Piazza di Spagna
& the Spanish Steps   PIAZZA
(Ⓜ Spagna) Piazza di Spagna was named after the Spanish Embassy to the Holy See, although the staircase, designed by the Italian Francesco de Sanctis and built in 1725 with a legacy from the French, leads to the French Chiesa della Trinità dei Monti. Rising above Piazza di Spagna, the Spanish Steps (Scalinata di Trinità dei Monti) are a favourite hang-out for footsore tourists, migrant hawkers and preening local teens. Come in the evening for a spot of people-watching: posing has a long and noble history here, and when Dickens visited in the 19th century he reported that artists' models would hang around in the hope of being hired for a painting. At the foot of the steps, the Barcaccia (the 'sinking boat' fountain) is believed to be by Pietro Bernini, father of the more famous Gian Lorenzo.

Trevi Fountain   FOUNTAIN
(Fontana di Trevi; Piazza di Trevi; Ⓜ Barberini) The Fontana di Trevi, scene of Anita Ekberg's dip in *La Dolce Vita*, is a flamboyant baroque ensemble of mythical figures and wild horses. It takes up the entire side of the 17th-century Palazzo Poli. A Fendi-sponsored restoration finished in 2015, and the fountain now gleams brighter than it has for years.

The tradition is to toss a coin into the water, thus ensuring that you'll return to Rome.

St Peter's Basilica   BASILICA
(Basilica di San Pietro; www.vatican.va; St Peter's Sq; ⊙ 7am-7pm summer, to 6.30pm winter; Ⓜ Ottaviano-San Pietro) In a city of outstanding churches, none hold a candle to St Peter's Basilica, Italy's biggest, richest and most spectacular cathedral. It contains some brilliant artworks, including three of Rome's most celebrated masterpieces: Michelangelo's *Pietà*, his breathtaking dome, and Bernini's baldachin (canopy) over the papal altar.

ROME SIGHTS

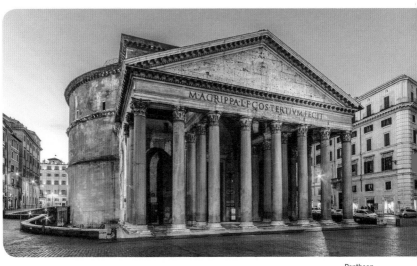

Pantheon

Rome

Vatican Museums   MUSEUM

(Musei Vaticani; 📞 06 6988 4676; http://mv.vatican.
va; Viale Vaticano; adult/reduced €16/8, last Sun of
month free; ⏱ 9am-4pm Mon-Sat, 9am-12.30pm
last Sun of month; Ⓜ Ottaviano-San Pietro) Visiting
the Vatican Museums is a thrilling and unforgettable experience. The highlight is the
Michelangelo-decorated Sistine Chapel, but
with some 7km of exhibitions and more masterpieces than many small countries, there's
enough art on display to keep you busy for
years. Housing it all is the 5.5-hectare Palazzo

Rome

Apostolico Vaticano, which also serves as the pope's official residence.

Museo Nazionale Romano: Palazzo Massimo alle Terme   MUSEUM

(☑ 06 3996 7700; www.coopculture.it; Largo di Villa Peretti 1; adult/reduced €7/3.50; ◉ 9am-7.45pm Tue-Sun; Ⓜ Termini) One of Rome's great unheralded museums, this is a fabulous treasure trove of classical art. The ground and 1st floors are devoted to sculpture with some breathtaking pieces – check out the *Pugile* (Boxer), a 2nd-century-BC Greek bronze; the graceful 2nd-century-BC *Ermafrodite dormiente* (Sleeping Hermaphrodite); and the idealised *Il discobolo* (Discus Thrower). It's the magnificent and vibrantly coloured frescoes on the 2nd floor, however, that are the undisputed highlight.

Basilica di Santa Maria in Trastevere   BASILICA

(Piazza Santa Maria in Trastevere; ◉ 7.30am-9pm; ☐ Viale di Trastevere, ☐ Viale di Trastevere) Nestled in a quiet corner of Trastevere's focal square, this is said to be the oldest church

dedicated to the Virgin Mary in Rome. In its original form it dates to the early 3rd century, but a major 12th-century makeover saw the addition of a Romanesque bell tower and glittering facade. The portico came later, added by Carlo Fontana in 1702. Inside, the 12th-century mosaics are the headline feature.

Basilica di San Giovanni in Laterano   BASILICA

(Piazza di San Giovanni in Laterano 4; basilica/cloister free/€5; ◉ 7am-6.30pm, cloister 9am-6pm; Ⓜ San Giovanni) For a thousand years this monumental cathedral was the most important church in Christendom. Commissioned by Constantine and consecrated in AD 324, it was the first Christian basilica built in the city and, until the late 14th century, was the pope's main place of worship. It's still Rome's official cathedral and the pope's seat as the bishop of Rome.

Museo e Galleria Borghese   MUSEUM

(☑ 06 3 28 10; www.galleriaborghese.it; Piazzale del Museo Borghese 5; adult/reduced €11/6.50;

⊙9am-7pm Tue-Sun; 🚇Via Pinciana) If you only have the time, or inclination, for one art gallery in Rome, make it this one. Housing the 'queen of all private art collections', including works by Caravaggio, Bernini, Botticelli and Raphael, it provides the perfect introduction to Renaissance and baroque art without ever being overwhelming. Visitors are admitted at two-hourly intervals, so you'll need to call to prebook, and then enter at an allotted time. Trust us, though, it's worth it.

Via Appia Antica   HISTORIC SITE
(Appian Way; ☎06 513 53 16; www.parcoappia antica.it; bike hire hr/day €3/15; ⊙Info Point 9.30am-1pm & 2-5.30pm Mon-Fri, 9.30am-6.30pm Sat & Sun, to 5pm winter; 🚇Via Appia Antica) Named after consul Appius Claudius Caecus who laid the first 90km section in 312 BC, ancient Rome's *regina viarum* (queen of roads) was extended in 190 BC to reach Brindisi on Italy's southern Adriatic coast. Via Appia Antica has long been one of Rome's most exclusive addresses, a beautiful cobbled thoroughfare flanked by grassy fields, Roman structures and towering pine trees. Most splendid of the ancient houses was Villa dei Quintili, so desirable that Emperor Commodus murdered its owners and took it for himself.

🍴 Courses

Roman Kitchen   COOKING
(☎06 678 57 59; www.italiangourmet.com; per day €200) Cookery writer Diane Seed *(The Top One Hundred Pasta Sauces)* runs cooking courses from her kitchen in Palazzo Doria Pamphilj. There are one-day, two-day, three-day and week-long courses costing €200 per day and €1000 per week.

Vino Roma   WINE COURSE
(☎328 4874497; www.vinoroma.com; Via in Selci 84/G; 2hr tastings per person €50) With beautifully appointed 1000-year-old cellars and a chic tasting studio, Vino Roma guides novices and experts in tasting wine, under the stewardship of sommelier Hande Leimer and his expert team. It also offers a wine-and-cheese dinner (€60), with snacks, cheeses and cold cuts to accompany the wines, and bespoke three-hour food tours. Book online.

👉 Tours

Roman Guy   TOUR
(theromanguy.com) A professional set-up that organises a wide range of group and private tours. Packages, led by English-speaking experts, include early-bird visits to the Vatican Museums (US$84), foodie tours of Trastevere and the Jewish Ghetto (US$84), and a bar hop through the historic centre's cocktail bars.

Eating Italy Food Tours   FOOD TOUR
(www.eatingitalyfoodtours.com; €75; ⊙daily) This cheery food tour company is run by American ex-pat Kenny Dunn, and offers informative four-hour tours around Testaccio (the

heartland of traditional Roman cooking), or Trastevere, with chances to taste 12 delicacies on the way. There is a maximum of 12 people to a tour.

Top Bike Rental & Tours
BICYCLE TOUR

(☑06 488 28 93; www.topbikerental.com; Via Labicana 49; ☺10am-7pm) Offers a series of bike tours throughout the city, including a four-hour 16km exploration of the city centre (€45) and an all-day 30km ride through Via Appia Antica and its environs (€79). Out-of-town tours take in Castel Gandolfo, Civita di Bagnoregio and Orvieto.

🛏 Sleeping

Beehive
HOSTEL €

(☑06 4470 4553; www.the-beehive.com; Via Marghera 8; dm €25-35, s €50-80, d €90-100, without bathroom s €60-70, d €70-80, tr €95-105; ❋ 🛜; Ⓜ Termini) 🌠 More boutique chic than backpacker dive, the Beehive is Rome's best hostel; book well ahead. There's a spotless, eight-person mixed dorm and six private double rooms, some with air-con. Original artworks and funky modular furniture add colour, plus there's a cafe. Some bright, well-cared-for off-site rooms, sharing communal bathrooms and kitchen, are also a bargain (single €40 to €50, double €60 to €80).

Althea Inn
B&B €

(☑339 4353717, 06 9893 2666; www.altheainn. com; Via dei Conciatori 9; d €70-125; Ⓜ Piramide) In a workaday apartment block, this friendly B&B offers superb value for money and easy access to Testaccio's bars, clubs and restaurants. Its spacious, light-filled rooms sport a modish look with white walls and tasteful modern furniture. Each also has a small terrace.

Palm Gallery Hotel
HOTEL €€

(☑06 6478 1859; www.palmgalleryhotel.com; Via delle Alpi 15d; s €100-120, d €100-210; ❋ 🛜; 🚌 Via Nomentana, 🚌 Viale Regina Margherita) Housed in an early-20th-century villa, this gorgeous hotel sports an eclectic look that effortlessly blends African and Middle Eastern art with original art-deco furniture, exposed brickwork and hand-painted tiles. Rooms are individually decorated, with the best offering views over the wisteria and thick greenery in the surrounding streets.

Residenza Maritti
GUESTHOUSE €€

(☑06 678 82 33; www.residenzamaritti.com; Via Tor de' Conti 17; s €50-120, d €80-170, tr €100-190; ❋ 🛜; Ⓜ Cavour) Boasting stunning views

over the forums, this gem has rooms spread over several floors. Some are bright and modern, others are more cosy in feel with antiques and family furniture. There's no breakfast but you can use a fully equipped kitchen.

Arco del Lauro
B&B €€

(☑346 2443212, 9am-2pm 06 9784 0350; www. arcodellauro.it; Via Arco de' Tolomei 27; s €72-132, d €132-145; ❋ 🛜; 🚌 Viale di Trastevere, 🚌 Viale di Trastevere) A real find, this fab six-room B&B occupies a centuries-old *palazzo* on a narrow cobbled street. Its gleaming white rooms combine rustic charm with a modern low-key look and comfortable beds. The owners extend a warm welcome and are always ready to help.

Villa Laetitia
BOUTIQUE HOTEL €€€

(☑06 322 67 76; www.villalaetitia.com; Lungotevere delle Armi 22; r €200-280, ste €500; ❋ 🛜; 🚌 Lungotevere delle Armi) Villa Laetitia is a stunning boutique hotel in a riverside art-nouveau villa. Its 20 rooms, each individually designed by Anna Venturini Fendi of the famous fashion house, marry modern design touches with vintage pieces and rare finds, such as an original Picasso in the Garden Room.

Villa Spalletti Trivelli
HOTEL €€€

(☑06 4890 7934; www.villaspalletti.it; Via Piacenza 4; r €450-620; ❋ @ 🛜; Ⓜ Spagna) With 12 rooms in a glorious mansion in central Rome, Villa Spalletti Trivelli was built by Gabriella Rasponi, widow of Italian senator Count Venceslao Spalletti Triveli and the niece of Carolina Bonaparte (Napoleon's sister). It offers a soujourn in a stately home: rooms are soberly and elegantly decorated, and the sitting rooms are hung with 16th-century tapestries or lined by antique books. There's a basement spa.

Donna Camilla Savelli
HOTEL €€€

(☑06 58 88 61; www.hoteldonnacamillasavelli.com; Via Garibaldi 27; d €165-250; ❋ @ 🛜; 🚌 Viale di Trastevere, 🚌 Viale di Trastevere) It's seldom you have such an exquisite opportunity as to stay in a converted convent that was designed by baroque genius Borromini. It's been beautifully updated; muted colours complement the serene concave and convex curves of the architecture, and service is excellent. The pricier of the 78 rooms overlook the lovely cloister garden, or have views of Rome, and are decorated with antiques – it's worth forking out that bit extra.

MENU DECODER

The hallmark of an authentic Roman menu is the presence of offal. The Roman love of nose-to-tail eating arose in Testaccio around the city abattoir, and many of the neighbourhood's trattorias still serve traditional offal-based dishes. So whether you want to avoid it or try it, look out for *pajata* (veal's intestines), *trippa* (tripe), *coda alla vaccinara* (oxtail), *coratella* (heart, lung and liver), *animelle* (sweetbreads), *testarella* (head), *lingua* (tongue) and *zampone* (trotters).

Eating

Supplizio
FAST FOOD €

(Via dei Banchi Vecchi 143; supplì €3-5; ⊘noon-4pm Mon-Sat plus 5.30-10pm Mon-Thu, to 11pm Fri & Sat; 🚇Corso Vittorio Emanuele II) Rome's favourite snack, the *supplì* (a fried croquette filled with rice, tomato sauce and mozzarella), gets a gourmet makeover at this elegant new street-food joint. Sit back on the vintage leather sofa and dig into the classic article or throw the boat out and try something different, maybe a mildly spicy fish *supplì* stuffed with anchovies, tuna, parsley, and just a hint of orange.

Cafè Cafè
BISTRO €

(🖉06 700 87 43; www.cafecafebistrot.it; Via dei Santissimi Quattro Coronati 44; meals €15-20; ⊘9.30am-11pm; 🚇Via di San Giovanni in Laterano) Cosy, relaxed and welcoming, this cafe-bistro is a far cry from the usual impersonal eateries in the Colosseum area. With its rustic wooden tables, butternut walls and wine bottles, it's a charming spot to recharge your batteries over tea and homemade cake, a light lunch or a laid-back dinner. There's also brunch on Sundays.

Terre e Domus
LAZIO CUISINE €€

(🖉06 6994 0273; Via Foro Traiano 82-4; meals €30; ⊘7.30am-12.30am Mon-Sat; 🚇Via dei Fori Imperiali) This modern white-and-glass restaurant is the best option in the touristy Forum area. Overlooking the Colonna di Traiano, it serves a menu of traditional staples, all made with ingredients sourced from the surrounding Lazio region, and a thoughtful selection of regional wines. Lunchtime can be busy but it quietens down in the evening.

La Ciambella
ITALIAN €€

(www.laciambellaroma.com; Via dell'Arco della Ciambella 20; fixed-price lunch menus €10-25, meals €30; ⊘7.30am-midnight; 🚇Largo di Torre Argentina) From breakfast pastries and lunchtime pastas to afternoon tea, Neapolitan pizzas and aperitif cocktails, this all-day eatery is a top find. Central but as yet undiscovered by the tourist hordes, it's a spacious, light-filled spot set over the ruins of the Terme di Agrippa, visible through transparent floor panels. The mostly traditional food is spot on, and the atmosphere laid back and friendly.

Enoteca Regionale Palatium
RISTORANTE, WINE BAR €€€

(🖉06 692 02 132; Via Frattina 94; meals €55; ⊘11am-11pm Mon-Sat, closed Aug; 🚇Via del Corso) A rich showcase of regional bounty, run by the Lazio Regional Food Authority, this sleek wine bar serves excellent local specialities, such as *porchetta* (pork roasted with herbs) or *gnocchi alla Romana con crema da zucca* (potato dumplings Roman-style with cream of pumpkin), as well as an array of Lazio wines (try lesser-known drops such as Aleatico). *Aperitivo* are a good bet, too.

Open Colonna
ITALIAN €€€

See p27

Drinking & Nightlife

0,75
BAR

(www.075roma.com; Via dei Cerchi 65; ⊘11am-2am; 🛜; 🚇Via dei Cerchi) This welcoming bar on the Circo Massimo is good for a lingering drink, an *aperitivo* (6.30pm onwards) or a light meal (mains €6 to €13.50, salads €5.50 to €7.50). It's a friendly place with a laid-back vibe, an attractive exposed-brick look and cool tunes.

Barnum Cafe
CAFE

(www.barnumcafe.com; Via del Pellegrino 87; ⊘9am-10pm Mon, 8.30am-2am Tue-Sat; 🛜; 🚇Corso Vittorio Emanuele II) A relaxed, friendly spot to check your email over a freshly squeezed orange juice, or to spend a pleasant hour reading a newspaper on one of the tatty old armchairs in the white bare-brick interior. Come evenings and the scene is cocktails, smooth tunes and coolly dressed-down locals.

No.Au
BAR

(Piazza Montevecchio 16; ⊘6pm-1am Tue-Thu, noon-1am Fri-Sun; 🚇Corso del Rinascimento) Opening on to a charming *centro storico* piazza,

No.Au – pronounced Know How – is a cool bistrot-bar set-up. Like many fashionable bars, it's big on beer and offers a knowledgeable list of artisanal craft brews, as well as local wines and a small but select food menu.

Sciascia Caffè
CAFE

(Via Fabio Massimo 80/A; ⊘ 7.30am-6.30pm Mon-Sat; Ⓜ Ottaviano–San Pietro) The timeless elegance of this polished cafe is perfectly suited to the exquisite coffee it makes. There are various options but nothing can beat the *caffè eccellente,* a velvety smooth espresso served in a delicate cup that has been lined with melted chocolate. The result is nothing short of magnificent.

Il Tiaso
BAR

(☑ 06 4547 4625; www.iltiaso.com; Via Perugia 20; 🖥; 🚊 Circonvallazione Casilina) Think living room with zebra-print chairs, walls of indie art, Lou Reed biographies shelved between wine bottles, and 30-something owner Gabriele playing his latest New York Dolls album to neo-beatnik chicks, corduroy professors and the odd neighbourhood dog. Well-priced wine, an intimate chilled vibe, and regular live music.

Goa
CLUB

(☑ 06 574 82 77; www.goaclub.com; Via Libetta 13; ⊘ 11.30pm-4.30am Thu-Sat; Ⓜ Garbatella) Goa is Rome's serious super-club, with international names, a fashion-forward crowd, podium dancers and heavies on the door.

🔒 Shopping

Confetteria Moriondo & Gariglio
FOOD

(Via del Piè di Marmo 21-22; ⊘ 9am-7.30pm Mon-Sat; 🚊 Via del Corso) Roman poet Trilussa was so smitten with this historic chocolate shop that he dedicated several sonnets to it. And we agree, it's a gem. Many of the bonbons and handmade chocolates laid out in ceremonial splendour in the glass cabinets are still prepared according to original 19th-century recipes.

Ibiz – Artigianato in Cuoio
ACCESSORIES

(Via dei Chiavari 39; ⊘ 9.30am-7.30pm Mon-Sat; 🚊 Corso Vittorio Emanuele II) In their diminutive workshop, Elisa Nepi and her father craft exquisite, well-priced leather goods, including wallets, bags, belts and sandals, in simple but classy designs and myriad colours.

Officina Profumo Farmaceutica di Santa Maria Novella
BEAUTY

See p27

Bottega di Marmoraro
ARTS

(Via Margutta 53b; ⊘ 8am-7.30pm Mon-Sat; Ⓜ Flaminio) A particularly charismatic hole-in-the-wall shop lined with marble carvings, where you can get marble tablets engraved with any inscription you like (€15).

Danielle
SHOES

(☑ 06 679 24 67; Via Frattina 85a; ⊘ 10.30am-7.30pm; Ⓜ Spagna) For women's shoes this is

Al fresco dining, Campo de'Fiori

an essential stop on your itinerary. It sells both classic and fashionable styles – foxy heels, boots and ballet pumps – at extremely reasonable prices. Shoes are of soft leather and come in myriad colours.

Tina Sondergaard CLOTHING
(☑ 334 3850799; Via del Boschetto 1d; ⊘ 3-7.30pm Mon, 10.30am-7.30pm Tue-Sat, closed Aug; Ⓜ Cavour) Sublimely cut and whimsically retro, these handmade threads are a hit with female fashion cognoscenti. You can have adjustments made (included in the price), and dresses cost around €140.

Porta Portese Market MARKET
(Piazza Porta Portese; ⊘ 6am-2pm Sun; 🚊 Viale di Trastevere, 🚊 Viale di Trastevere) To see another side of Rome, head to this mammoth flea market. With thousands of stalls selling everything from rare books and fell-off-a-lorry bikes to Peruvian shawls and MP3 players, it's crazily busy and a lot of fun. Keep your valuables safe.

❶ Orientation

Rome is a sprawling city but the centre is relatively compact and most sights are concentrated in the area between Stazione Termini, the city's main transport hub, and the Vatican to the west. Halfway between the two, the Pantheon and Piazza Navona lie at the heart of the *centro storico*, while to the south, the Colosseum lords it over the city's great ancient ruins: the Roman Forum and Palatino. On the west bank of the Tiber, St Peter's Basilica trumpets the presence of the Vatican.

Distances are not great so walking is often the best way to get around.

❶ Information

MEDICAL SERVICES

For problems that don't require hospital treatment, call the **Guardia Medica** (☑ 06 884 01 13; Via Mantova 44; ⊘ 24 hr).

More convenient, if you have insurance and can afford to pay up front, is to call a doctor for a home visit. Try the **International Medical Centre** (☑ 06 488 23 71; Via Firenze 47; GP call-out & treatment fee €140, 8pm-9am & weekends €200; ⊘ 24hr).

TOURIST INFORMATION

For phone enquiries, the Comune di Roma runs a free multilingual **tourist information line** (☑ 06 06 08; ⊘ 9am-9pm).

USEFUL WEBSITES

060608 (www.060608.it) Information on sites, accommodation, shows, transport.
Coop Culture (www.coopculture.it) Information and ticketing for Rome's monuments, museums and galleries.
In Rome Now (www.inromenow.com) Savvy internet magazine from two American expats.
Turismo Roma (www.turismoroma.it) Rome's official tourist website. Lists accommodation options, upcoming events and more.
Vatican (www.vatican.va) The Vatican's website.

❶ Getting There & Around

AIR

Rome's main international airport, Leonardo da Vinci (p121), better known as Fiumicino, is on the coast 30km west of the city.

The much smaller **Ciampino Airport** (☑ 06 6 59 51; www.adr.it/ciampino), 15km southeast of the city centre, is the hub for European low-cost carrier Ryanair.

MUSEUM DISCOUNT CARDS

Serious museum-goers should consider the following:

➡ **Classic Roma Pass** (€36; valid for three days) Provides free admission to two museums or sites, as well as reduced entry to extra sites, unlimited city transport and discounted entry to other exhibitions and events.

➡ **48-hour Roma Pass** (€28; valid for 48 hours) Gives free admission to one museum or site and then as per the classic pass.

➡ **Archaeologia Card** (adult/reduced €27.50/17.50; valid for seven days) Covers the Colosseum, Palatino, Roman Forum, Terme di Caracalla, Palazzo Altemps, Palazzo Massimo alle Terme, Terme di Diocleziano, Crypta Balbi, Mausoleo di Cecilia Metella and Villa dei Quintili.

These are all available at participating museums or online at www.coopculture.it. You can also get the Roma Pass at tourist information points.

CAR & MOTORCYCLE

Driving into central Rome is a challenge, involving traffic restrictions, one-way systems, a shortage of street parking and aggressive drivers.

Rome is circled by the *Grande Raccordo Anulare* (GRA) to which all autostradas (motorways) connect, including the main A1 north–south artery (the Autostrada del Sole) and the A12, which runs to Civitavecchia and Fiumicino Airport.

Car Hire

Rental cars are available at the airport and Stazione Termini.

Avis (☑199 100 133; www.avisautonoleggio.it)
Europcar (☑199 30 70 30; www.europcar.it)
Hertz (☑02 6943 0019; www.hertz.it)
Maggiore National (☑199 151 120; www.maggiore.it)

Access & Parking

➡ Most of the historic centre is closed to unauthorised traffic from 6.30am to 6pm Monday to Friday, from 2pm to 6pm (10am to 7pm in some places) Saturday, and from 11pm to 3am Friday and Saturday. Evening restrictions also apply in Trastevere, San Lorenzo, Monti and Testaccio, typically from 9.30pm or 11pm to 3am on Fridays and Saturdays.

➡ All streets accessing the 'Limited Traffic Zone' (ZTL) are monitored by electronic-access detection devices. If you're staying in this zone, contact your hotel. For further information, check www.agenziamobilita.roma.it.

➡ Blue lines denote pay-and-display parking – get tickets from meters (coins only) or a *tabaccheria* (tobacconist's shop).

➡ Traffic wardens are vigilant and fines are not uncommon. If your car gets towed away, call ☑06 6769 2303.

➡ There's a comprehensive list of car parks at www.060608.it – click on the transport tab and car parks.

PUBLIC TRANSPORT

Rome's public transport system includes buses, trams, the metro and a suburban train network.

Metro

➡ Rome has two main metro lines, A (orange) and B (blue), which cross at Termini. A branch line, 'B1', serves the northern suburbs, and line C runs through the southeastern outskirts, but you're unlikely to need these.

➡ Trains run between 5.30am and 11.30pm (to 1.30am on Fridays and Saturdays).

➡ All stations on line B have wheelchair access except Circo Massimo, Colosseo and Cavour. On line A, Ottaviano–San Pietro and Termini are equipped with lifts.

➡ Take line A for the Trevi Fountain (Barberini), Spanish Steps (Spagna) and St Peter's (Ottaviano–San Pietro).

➡ Take line B for the Colosseum (Colosseo).

Bus & Tram

➡ Rome's buses and trams are run by **ATAC** (☑06 5 70 03; www.atac.roma.it).

➡ The main bus station is in front of Stazione Termini on Piazza dei Cinquecento, where there's an **information booth** (◷7.30am-8pm).

➡ Other important hubs are at Largo di Torre Argentina and Piazza Venezia.

➡ Buses generally run from about 5.30am until midnight, with limited services through the night.

➡ Rome's night bus service comprises more than 25 lines, many of which pass Termini and/or Piazza Venezia. Buses are marked with an 'n' before the number and bus stops have a blue owl symbol. Departures are usually every 15 to 30 minutes between about 1am and 5am, but can be much less frequent.

TAXI

➡ Official licensed taxis are white with an ID number and *Roma Capitale* on the sides.

➡ Always go with the metered fare, never an arranged price (the set fares to/from the airports are exceptions).

➡ In town (within the ring road) flag fall is €3 between 6am and 10pm on weekdays and Saturdays, €4.50 on Sundays and holidays, and €6.50 between 10pm and 6am. Then it's €1.10 per kilometre. Official rates are posted in taxis and on www.agenziamobilita.roma.it.

➡ You can hail a taxi, but it's often easier to wait at a rank or phone for one. There are taxi ranks at the airports, Stazione Termini, Piazza della Repubblica, Piazza Barberini, Piazza di Spagna, the Pantheon, the Colosseum, Largo di Torre Argentina, Piazza Belli, Piazza Pio XII and Piazza del Risorgimento.

➡ You can book a taxi by phoning the Comune di Roma's automated taxi line on ☑06 06 09 or by calling a taxi company direct.

➡ Note that when you call for a cab, the meter is switched on straight away and you pay for the cost of the journey from wherever the driver receives the call.

La Capitale (☑06 49 94)
Pronto Taxi (☑06 66 45)
Radio 3570 (☑06 35 70; www.3570.it)
Samarcanda (☑06 55 51; www.samarcanda.it)
Tevere (☑06 41 57)

ROME GETTING THERE & AROUND

Life is sweet around leading lady Florence, known for her truly extraordinary treasure trove of world-class art and architecture, and cuisine emulated the world over.

Florence

FLORENCE

POP 377,200

Controversy continues over the founding of Florence. Although the commonly accepted story tells us that Emperor Julius Caesar founded Florentia around 59 BC, there is archaeological evidence of an Etruscan village from around 200 BC. Over the centuries the city has known many different incarnations under different rulers. The influence of the wealthy Medici family in the 15th century lead to a flowering of art, music and poetry, turning Florence into Italy's cultural capital.

In 1737 control of Tuscany passed to the French House of Lorraine, which retained control, apart from a brief interruption under Napoleon, until it was incorporated into the Kingdom of Italy in 1860. Florence briefly became the national capital but Rome assumed the mantle permanently in 1870.

◉ Sights

Duomo   CATHEDRAL
(Map p70; Cattedrale di Santa Maria del Fiore; www.operaduomo.firenze.it; Piazza del Duomo; ⊙10am-5pm Mon-Wed & Fri, to 4.30pm Thu, to 4.45pm Sat, 1.30-4.45pm Sun) **FREE** Florence's Duomo is the city's most iconic landmark. Capped by a red-tiled cupola, it's a staggering construction whose breathtaking pink, white and green marble facade and

graceful *campanile* (bell tower) dominate the medieval cityscape. Sienese architect Arnolfo di Cambio began work on it 1296, but construction took almost 150 years and it wasn't consecrated until 1436. In the echoing interior, look out for frescoes by Vasari and Zuccari and look up to 44 stained-glass windows. The cupola is a feat of engineering and one that cannot be fully appreciated without climbing its 463 interior stone steps (adult/child incl campanile & baptistry €15/3). It was built between 1420 and 1436 to a design by Filippo Brunelleschi, and is a staggering 91m high and 45.5m wide. The 414-step climb up the cathedral's 85m-tall campanile, begun by Giotto in 1334, rewards with a staggering city panorama. The first tier of bas-reliefs around the base of its elaborate Gothic facade are copies of those carved by Pisano depicting the Creation of Man and the *attività umane* (arts and industries).

Palazzo Vecchio   MUSEUM
(Map p70; ☏055 276 82 24; www.musefirenze. it; Piazza della Signoria; museum & tower adult/ reduced €14/12; ⊙hours vary seasonally) This fortress palace was designed by Arnolfo di Cambio between 1298 and 1314 for the *signoria* (city government), and remains the seat of the city's power to this day. From the

Duomo

top of the **Torre d'Arnolfo** (tower), you can revel in unforgettable rooftop views. Inside, Michelangelo's *Genio della Vittoria* (Genius of Victory) sculpture graces the Salone dei Cinquecento, a magnificent painted hall created for the city's 15th-century ruling Consiglio dei Cinquecento (Council of 500).

Galleria degli Uffizi   GALLERY
(Map p70; Uffizi Gallery; www.uffizi.firenze.it; Piazzale degli Uffizi 6; adult/reduced €8/4, incl temporary exhibition €12.50/6.25; ⊙ 8.15am-6.50pm Tue-Sun) Home to the world's greatest collection of Italian Renaissance art, Florence's premier gallery occupies the vast U-shaped Palazzo degli Uffizi, built to house government offices. The collection, bequeathed to the city by the Medici family in 1743 on condition that it never leave Florence, contains some of Italy's best-known paintings including Piero della Francesco's profile portaits of the Duke and Duchess of Urbino and a room full of masterpieces by Sandro Botticelli, including *La nascita di Venere* (The Birth of Venus; c 1485), and *Primavera* (Spring; c 1482).

Museo del Bargello   MUSEUM
(Map p70; www.polomuseale.firenze.it; Via del Proconsolo 4; adult/reduced €4/2; ⊙ 8.15am-4.50pm summer, to 1.50pm winter, closed 1st, 3rd & 5th Sun & 2nd & 4th Mon of month) It was behind the stark walls of Palazzo del Bargello, Florence's earliest public building, that the podestà meted out justice from the late 13th century until 1502. Today the building safeguards Italy's most comprehensive collection of Tuscan Renaissance sculpture with some of Michelangelo's best early works and a hall full of Donatello's. Michelangelo was just 21 when a cardinal commissioned him to create the drunken grape-adorned *Bacchus* (1496–97), displayed in Bargello's downstairs Sala di Michelangelo.

> **ⓘ SAVVY ADVANCE PLANNING**
>
> ➡ To cut costs, visit on the first Sunday of the month when admission to state museums, including the Uffizi and Galleria dell'Accademia, is free.
>
> ➡ Cut queues by booking tickets in advance for the Uffizi and Galleria dell'Accademia.
>
> ➡ The Uffizi, Galleria dell'Accademia and most other state museums are shut on Monday – the perfect day for visiting the hidden gem of Museo di Orsanmichele.
>
> ➡ Reserve a tour of the Vasari corridor (on Ponte Vecchio) and tickets for Cappella Brancacci.
>
> ➡ Book family-friendly tours and/or art workshops at Palazzo Vecchio and Museo Novecento.
>
> ➡ Buy tickets for springtime's Maggio Musicale Fiorentino festival.

Florence

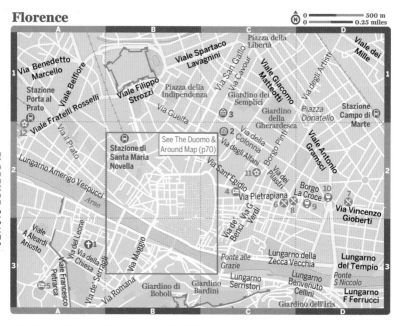

Florence

⊚ Sights
1 Cappella Brancacci	A3
2 Galleria dell'Accademia	C2
3 Museo di San Marco	C1

⊜ Sleeping
4 Hotel Dalì	C2
5 Ostello Tasso	A3

⊗ Eating
6 Il Teatro del Sale	C2
7 Osteria del Cocotrippone	D2
8 Pollini	C2

⊜ Drinking & Nightlife
9 Drogheria	D2
10 Kitsch	D2

⊛ Entertainment
11 Jazz Club	C2
12 Opera di Firenze	A2

Museo Novecento   MUSEUM

(Map p70; Museum of the 20th Century; ☑ 055 28 61 32; www.museonovecento.it; Piazza di Santa Maria Novella 10; adult/reduced €8.50/4; ⊙ 10am-6pm Mon-Wed, to 2pm Thu, to 9pm Fri, to 8pm Sat & Sun) Don't allow the Renaissance to distract from Florence's fantastic modern art museum, in a 13th-century *palazzo* previously used as a pilgrim shelter, hospital and school. A well-articulated itinerary guides visitors through modern Italian painting and sculpture from the early 20th century to the late 1980s. Installation art makes effective use of the outside space on the 1st-floor loggia. Fashion and theatre get a nod on the 2nd floor, and the itinerary ends with a 20-minute cinematic montage of the best films set in Florence.

Galleria dell'Accademia   GALLERY

(Map p68; www.polomuseale.firenze.it; Via Ricasoli 60; adult/reduced €8/4; ⊙ 8.15am-6.50pm Tue-Sun) A queue marks the door to this gallery, built to house one of the Renaissance's most iconic masterpieces, Michelangelo's *David*. But the world's most famous statue is worth the wait. The subtle detail of the real thing – the veins in his sinewy arms, the leg muscles, the change in expression as you move around the statue – *is* impressive.

Museo di San Marco   MUSEUM

(Map p68; see p44)

Cappella Brancacci   CHAPEL

See p44

Ponte Vecchio BRIDGE

(Map p74) Dating to 1345, Ponte Vecchio was the only Florentine bridge to survive destruction at the hands of retreating German forces in 1944. Above the jewellers' shops on the eastern side, the Corridoio Vasariano (Vasari corridor) is a 16th-century passageway between the Uffizi and Palazzo Pitti that runs around, rather than through, the medieval Torre dei Mannelli at the bridge's southern end. The first evidence of a stone bridge here, at the narrowest crossing point along the entire length of the Arno, dates from 972.

☞ Tours

City Sightseeing Firenze BUS TOUR

(Map p70; ☑ 055 29 04 51; www.firenze.city-sightseeing.it; Piazza della Stazione 1; adult 1/2/3 days €20/25/30) Explore Florence by red open-top bus, hopping on and off at 15 bus stops around the city. Tickets, sold by the driver, are valid for 24 hours.

De Gustibus TOUR

(☑ 340 579 62 07; www.de-gustibus.it) This umbrella association for farms in the surrounding Florentine countryside organises extremely tasty tours to small family-run organic farms. Tours are invariably themed – wine, truffles, olive oil – and can be by car, on foot or by bicycle. Check its website or Facebook page for details of upcoming tours.

ArtViva WALKING TOUR

(Map p70; ☑ 055 264 50 33; www.italy.artviva.com; Via de' Sassetti 1; per person from €25) One- to three-hour city walks led by historians or art history graduates: tours include the Uffizi, the Original David tour and an adult-only 'Sex, Drugs & the Renaissance' art tour.

★ Festivals & Events

Festa di Anna Maria Medici CULTURAL

(☉18 Feb) Florence's Feast of Anna Maria Medici marks the death in 1743 of the last Medici, Anna Maria, with a costumed parade from Palazzo Vecchio to her tomb in the Cappelle Medicee.

Maggio Musicale Fiorentino PERFORMING ARTS

(www.operadifirenze.it) Italy's oldest arts festival features world-class performances of theatre, classical music, jazz and dance; April to June.

Festa di San Giovanni RELIGIOUS

(☉24 Jun) Florence celebrates its patron saint, John, with a *calcio storico* (historic football) match on Piazza di Santa Croce and fireworks over Piazzale Michelangelo.

🛏 Sleeping

Florence is unexpectedly small, rendering almost anywhere in the centre convenient.

Hotel Dalí HOTEL €

(Map p68; ☑ 055 234 07 06; www.hoteldali.com; Via dell'Oriuolo 17; d €90, s/d without bathroom €40/70, apt from €95; P 🖂) A warm welcome from hosts Marco and Samanta awaits at this lovely small hotel. A stone's throw from the Duomo, it has 10 sunny rooms, some overlooking a leafy inner courtyard, decorated in a low-key modern way and equipped with kettles, coffee and tea. No breakfast, but – miraculous for downtown Florence – free parking in the rear courtyard.

Ostello Tasso HOSTEL €

(Map p68; ☑ 055 060 20 87; www.ostellotassofirenze.it; Via Villani 15; dm €30-32, s/d €37/70; @ 🖂) Hostelling in Florence got a whole load more stylish with the opening of this chic crash pad, a two-minute walk from the tasty eateries of Piazza Tasso. Coloured bed linen and floor rugs give three- to six-bed dorms a boutique charm, the courtyard garden is a

---

❶ PLAN AHEAD: THE FIRENZE CARD

The Firenze Card (www.firenzecard.it; €72) is valid for 72 hours and covers admission to some museums, villas and gardens in Florence, as well as unlimited use of public transport and free wifi across the city. Its biggest advantage is reducing queuing time in high season – museums have a separate queue for cardholders. The downside of the Firenze Card is it only allows one admission per museum, plus you need to visit an awful lot of museums to justify the cost.

Buy the card online (and collect upon arrival in Florence) or buy in Florence at tourist offices or ticketing desks of the Uffizi (Entrance 2), Palazzo Pitti, Palazzo Vecchio, Museo del Bargello, Cappella Brancacci, Basilica di Santa Maria Novella and Giardino Bardini. If you're an EU citizen, your card also covers under 18s travelling with you.

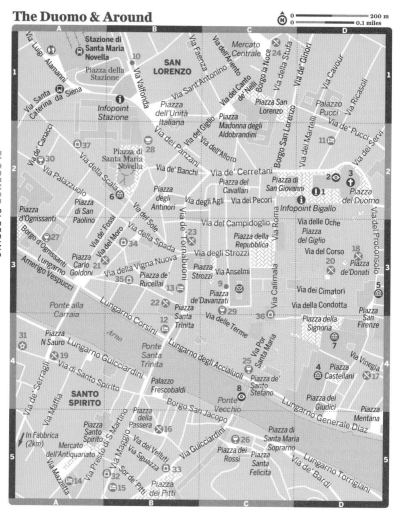

dream, and DJs spin tunes in the hip lounge bar (open to nonguests too). Rates include breakfast, locker, sheets and towel.

Academy Hostel   HOSTEL €

(Map p70; ☑ 055 239 86 65; www.academy hostel.eu; Via Ricasoli 9r; dm €32-36, s/d €42/100, d without bathroom €85; ❋ @ 🛜) This classy 10-room, 40-bed hostel sits on the 1st floor of Baron Ricasoli's 17th-century *palazzo*. The inviting lobby area was once a theatre and 'dorms' sport maximum four or six beds, high moulded ceilings and brightly coloured

lockers. The terrace is a perfect spot to chill. No credit cards for payments under €100.

Hotel Scoti   PENSION €€

(Map p70; ☑ 055 29 21 28; www.hotelscoti.com; Via de' Tornabuoni 7; s/d €75/130; 🛜) Wedged between the designer stores on Florence's smartest shopping strip, this hidden *pensione* is a splendid mix of old-fashioned charm and value for money. Its 16 traditionally styled rooms are spread across the 2nd floor of a towering 16th-century *palazzo*, with some offering lovely rooftop views.

The Duomo & Around

The star of the show, though, is the frescoed lounge from 1780. Breakfast €5.

Palazzo Guadagni Hotel HOTEL €€
(Map p70; ☏055 265 83 76; www.palazzogua dagni.com; Piazza Santo Spirito 9; d €150, extra bed €45; ❀⌨🅢) This romantic hotel overlooking Florence's liveliest summertime square is legendary – Zefferelli shot scenes from *Tea with Mussolini* here. Housed in a revamped Renaissance palace, it has 15 spacious if old-fashioned rooms and an impossibly romantic loggia terrace with wicker chairs and predictably dreamy views. Off season, double room rates drop as low as €90.

Antica Torre di Via de' Tornabuoni 1 BOUTIQUE HOTEL €€€
(Map p70; ☏055 265 81 61; www.tornabuoni1.com; Via de' Tornabuoni 1; d from €200; 🅢📶) Just steps from the Arno, inside the beautiful 14th-century Palazzo Gianfigliazzi, is this raved-about hotel. Its 20 rooms are stylish, spacious and contemporary. But what completely steals the show is the stunning roof-top breakfast terrace – easily the best in the city. Sip cappuccino and swoon over Florence graciously laid out at your feet.

SoprArno Suites GUESTHOUSE €€€
(Map p70; ☏055 046 87 18; www.soprarno suites.com; Via Maggio 35; d from €230; 🅢) A brilliant addition to the hotel scene, this boutique address squirrelled away in an Oltrarno courtyard creates an intimate home-from-home vibe while making it very clear each guest is special. Each of the 11 designer rooms ia exquisitely dressed in vintage objets d'art and collectables – the passion of Florentine owner Matteo and his talented Florence-born, British-raised wife Betty Soldi (herself a calligrapher and graphic designer).

✖ Eating

Quality ingredients and simple execution are the hallmarks of Florentine cuisine. Typical dishes include *crostini* (toast topped with chicken-liver pâté or other toppings), *ribollita* (a thick vegetable, bread and bean soup), *pappa al pomodoro* (bread and tomato soup) and *trippa alla fiorentina* (tripe cooked in a rich tomato sauce).

Mariano SANDWICHES €
(Map p70; Via del Parione 19r; panini €3-5; ☉8am-3pm & 5-7.30pm Mon-Fri, 8am-3pm Sat) Our favourite for its simplicity, around since 1973. Sunrise to sunset this brick-vaulted, 13th-century cellar gently buzzes with Florentines propped at the counter sipping coffee or wine or eating salads and *panini*. Come here for a coffee-and-pastry 71

breakfast, a light lunch, an *aperitivo* or a *panino* to eat on the move.

Look for the green neon 'pizzicheria' up high on the outside facade and the discreet 'alimentari' sign above the entrance.

Trattoria Mario
TUSCAN €

(Map p70; www.trattoria-mario.com; Via Rosina 2; meals €20; ☺noon-3.30pm Mon-Sat, closed 3 weeks Aug) Arrive by noon to ensure a stool around a shared table at this noisy, busy, brilliant trattoria – a legend that retains its soul (and allure with locals) despite being in every guidebook. Charming Fabio, whose grandfather opened the place in 1953, is front of house while big brother Romeo and nephew Francesco cook with speed in the kitchen.

Monday and Thursday are tripe days, and Friday is fish. Whatever the day, local Florentines flock here for a brilliantly blue *bistecca alla fiorentina*. No advance reservations, no credit cards.

All'Antico Vinaio
OSTERIA €

(Map p70; ☑ 055 238 27 23; www.allantico vinaio.com; Via dei Neri 65r; tasting platters €8-30, focaccias €5-7; ☺10am-4pm & 6-11pm Tue-Sat, noon-3.30pm Sun) The crowd spills out the door of this noisy Florentine thoroughbred. Push your way to the tables at the back and pray for a pew to taste cheese and salami in situ. Or join the queue at the deli counter for a well-stuffed focaccia to take away – the quality is outstanding. Pour yourself a glass of wine (€2) while you wait.

5 e Cinque
VEGETARIAN €

(Map p70; ☑ 055 274 15 83; Piazza della Passera 1; meals €25; ☺10am-10pm Tue-Sun) The hard work

and passion of a photographer and antique dealer is behind this highly creative, intimate eating space adored by every savvy local. Cuisine is vegetarian with its roots in Genoa's kitchen – '5 e Cinque' (meaning '5 and 5') is a chickpea sandwich from Livorno and the restaurant's *cecina* (traditional Ligurian flat bread made from chickpea flour) is legendary.

Obicà
ITALIAN €€

(Map p70; ☑ 055 277 35 26; www.obica.com; Via de' Tornabuoni 16; 1/2/3 mozzarella €13/20/30, pizza €9.50-17, tagliere €4.50-19.50; ☺noon-4pm & 6.30-11.30pm Mon-Fri, noon-11pm Sat & Sun) Given its exclusive location in Palazzo Tornabuoni, this designer address is naturally ubertrendy – even the table mats are upcycled from organic products. Taste different mozzarella cheeses in the cathedral-like interior or snuggle beneath heaters on sofa seating in the elegant, star-topped courtyard. At *aperitivo* hour nibble on *tagliere* (tasting boards loaded with cheeses, salami, deep fried veg and so on).

Il Teatro del Sale
TUSCAN €€

(Map p68; ☑ 055 200 14 92; www.teatrodelsale. com; Via dei Macci 111r; lunch/dinner/weekend brunch €15/20/30; ☺11am-3pm & 7.30-11pm Tue-Sat, 11am-3pm Sun, closed Aug) Florentine chef Fabio Picchi is one of Florence's living treasures, and he steals the Sant'Ambrogio show with this eccentric, good-value members-only club (everyone welcome, annual membership €7) inside an old theatre. He cooks up weekend brunch, lunch and dinner, culminating at 9.30pm in a live performance of drama, music or comedy arranged by his wife, artistic director and comic actress Maria Cassi.

TRIPE: FAST-FOOD FAVOURITE

When Florentines fancy a fast munch on the move, they flit by a *trippaio* – a cart on wheels or mobile stand – for a tripe *panino* (sandwich). Think cow's stomach chopped up, boiled, sliced, seasoned and bunged between bread.

Bastions of good old-fashioned Florentine tradition, *trippai* still going strong include the cart on the southwest corner of Mercato Nuovo (p74), L'Antico Trippaio (Map p70; Piazza dei Cimatori; ☺vary), Pollini (Map p68; Piazza Sant'Ambrogio; ☺variable) and hole-in-the-wall Da Vinattieri (Map p70; Via Santa Margherita 4; panini €4.50; ☺10am-7.30pm Mon-Fri, to 8pm Sat & Sun). Pay up to €4.50 for a *panino* with tripe doused in *salsa verde* (pea-green sauce of smashed parsley, garlic, capers and anchovies) or garnished with salt, pepper and ground chilli. Alternatively, opt for a bowl (€5.50 to €7) of *lampredotto* (cow's fourth stomach chopped and simmered for hours).

The pew-style seating at staunchly local Osteria del Cocotrippone (Map p68; ☑ 055 234 75 27; Via Vincenzo Gioberti 140; meals €25; ☺noon-2.30pm & 7-10.30pm) in the off-centre Beccaria neighbourhood is not a coincidence: Florentines come here to venerate the offal side of their city's traditional cuisine. The *trippa alla fiorentina* (tripe in tomato sauce) and *L'Intelligente* (fried brain and courgette) are local legends.

Il Santo Bevitore
TUSCAN €€

(Map p70; ☑ 055 21 12 64; www.ilsantobevi tore.com; Via di Santo Spirito 64-66r; meals €40; ⏰ 12.30-2.30pm & 7.30-11pm, closed Aug) Reserve or arrive dot-on 7.30pm to snag the last table at this ever-popular address, an ode to stylish dining where gastronomes dine by candlelight in a vaulted, whitewashed, bottle-lined interior. The menu is a creative re-invention of seasonal classics, different for lunch and dinner: purple cabbage soup with mozzarella cream and anchovy syrup, acacia honey *bavarese* (firm, creamy mousse) with Vin Santo–marinated dried fruits.

L'Osteria di Giovanni
TUSCAN €€€

(Map p70; ☑ 055 28 48 97; www.osteriadigio vanni.it; Via del Moro 22; meals €50; ⏰ 7-10pm Mon-Fri, noon-3pm & 7-10pm Sat & Sun) Cuisine at this smart neighbourhood eatery is sumptuously Tuscan. Imagine truffles, tender steaks and pastas such as *pici al sugo di salsiccia e cavolo nero* (thick spaghetti with a sauce of sausage and black cabbage). Throw in a complimentary glass of *prosecco* and you'll want to return time and again.

🍷 Drinking & Nightlife

Florence's drinking scene is split between *enoteche* (increasingly hip wine bars that invariably make great eating addresses too), trendy lounge bars with lavish *aperitivo* buffets (predinner drinks with nibbles from around 7pm to 10pm) and straightforward cafes that double as lovely lunch venues.

La Terrazza
BAR

(Map p70; www.continentale.it; Vicolo dell'Oro 6r; ⏰ 2.30-11.30pm Apr-Sep) This rooftop bar with wooden-decking terrace accessible from the 5th floor of the Ferragamo-owned Hotel Continentale is as chic as one would expect of a fashion-house hotel. Its *aperitivo* buffet is a modest affair, but who cares with that fabulous, drop-dead-gorgeous panorama of one of Europe's most beautiful cities. Dress the part or feel out of place.

Slowly
LOUNGE, BAR

(Map p70; www.slowlycafe.com; Via Porta Rossa 63r; ⏰ 6.30pm-3am Mon-Sat, closed Aug) Sleek and sometimes snooty, this lounge bar with a candle flickering on every table is known for its glam interior, Florentine Lotharios and lavish fruit-garnished cocktails – €10 including buffet during the bewitching *aperitivo* 'hour' (6.30pm to 10pm). Ibiza-style lounge tracks dominate the turntable.

SILVER SPOON DINING

In Fabbrica (☑ 347 5145468; www.pam-paloni.com; Via del Gelsomino 99; meals €45; ⏰ 8-10.30pm Wed-Sat), 1.5km south of Porto Romana along Via Senese on the Oltrarno, fuses Florence's outstanding tradition of fine craft with its equally fine cuisine. Meaning 'In the Factory', In Fabbrica is just that. By day, workers from third-generation Florentine silver house Pampaloni lunch here. Come dusk, the speakeasy canteen opens its doors to culturally curious diners.

Tables are laid with silver cutlery and majestic candelabras, waiters wear white gloves, and there are two fixed menus – one Italian, one Japanese. Advance reservations essential.

Shake Café
CAFE

(Map p70; ☑ 055 29 53 10; www.shakecafe.bio; Via degli Avelli 2r; ⏰ 7am-8pm) Handily close to the train station, this self-service juice bar has a perfect people-watching pavement terrace on car-free Piazza Santa Maria Novella. Its juices and smoothies include fabulous combos such as pineapple, fennel, celery, mint, chicory and liquorice. Unusually for Florence, Shake Café also makes cappuccinos with soya, almond or rice milk. Salads, wraps, sandwiches and gelati stave off hunger pangs.

Sei Divino
WINE BAR

(Map p70; Borgo d'Ognissanti 42r; ⏰ 6pm-2am Wed-Mon) This stylish wine bar tucked beneath a red-brick vaulted ceiling is privy to one of Florence's most happening *aperitivo* scenes. It plays music, hosts occasional exhibitions and in summertime the pavement action kicks in. *Aperitivo* 'hour' (with copious banquet) runs 7pm to 10pm.

Space Club
CLUB

(Map p70; www.spaceclubfirenze.com; Via Palazzuolo 37r; admission incl 1 drink €16; ⏰ 10pm-4am) Sheer size alone impresses at this vast club in Santa Maria Novella – dancing, drinking, video-karaoke in the bar, and a mixed student-international crowd.

Kitsch
BAR

(Map p68; www.kitschfirenze.com; Viale A Gramsci 5; ⏰ 6.30pm-2.30am; ☎) Cent-conscious Florentines love this American-styled bar for its lavish spread at *aperitivi* time – €10 for a drink and sufficient nibbles to not need dinner. It sports a dark-red theatrical interior and a bright 20s- to early-30s crowd out for a good time. DJ sets set the place rocking after dark. **Kitsch Devx** (Via San Gallo 22r; ☉6pm-2am) is its twin sister.

Drogheria
LOUNGE, BAR

(Map p68; www.drogheriafirenze.it; Largo Annigoni 22; ☉10am-2am) Be it rain, hail or shine, this is a lovely contemporary address in Santa Croce. Inside, it is a large space with dark wood furnishings and comfy leaf-green armchairs, perfect for lounging for hours on end. Come spring, the action moves outside onto the terrace, aplomb on the huge square across from Sant'Ambrogio market.

Le Volpi e l'Uva
WINE BAR

(Map p70; www.levolpieluva.com; Piazza dei Rossi 1; ☉11am-9pm Mon-Sat) This unasuming wine bar hidden away by Chiesa di Santa Felicità remains as appealing as it was the day it opened over a decade ago. Its food and wine pairings are first-class – taste and buy boutique wines by 150 small producers from all over Italy, matched perfectly with cheeses, cold meats and the best *crostini* in town. Wine-tasting classes too.

☆ Entertainment

La Cité
LIVE MUSIC

(Map p70; www.lacitelibreria.info; Borgo San Frediano 20r; ☉8am-2am Mon-Sat, 3pm-2am Sun; 🛜) A hip cafe-bookshop with an eclectic choice of vintage seating, La Cité makes a wonderful, intimate venue for live music – jazz, swing, world music – and book readings.

Jazz Club
JAZZ

(Map p68; Via Nuovo de' Caccini 3; ☉10.30pm-2am Tue-Sat, closed Jul & Aug) Catch salsa, blues, Dixieland and world music as well as jazz at Florence's top jazz venue.

Opera di Firenze
OPERA

(Map p68; ☏055 277 93 50; www.operadifirenze. it; Piazzale Vittorio Gui, Viale Fratelli Rosselli; ☉box office 2-6pm Mon, 10am-6pm Tue-Sat) Florence's striking new opera house with a glittering contemporary geometric facade sits on the green edge of city park Parco delle Cascine. Its three thoughtfully designed and multifunctional concert halls seat an audience of 5000 and play host to the springtime Maggio Musicale Fiorentino.

🛍 Shopping

Tacky mass-produced souvenirs are everywhere in Florence, not least at the city's two main markets, **Mercato Centrale** (www. mercatocentrale.it; Piazza del Mercato Centrale 4; ☉10am-1am, food stalls noon-3pm & 7pm-midnight) and **Mercato Nuovo** (Map p70; Loggia Mercato Nuovo; ☉8.30am-7pm Mon-Sat). But for serious shoppers keen to delve into a city synonymous with artisanship since medieval times, there are plenty of workshops and boutiques to visit. Leather goods, jewellery, hand-embroidered linens, designer fashion, per-

JOHN FREEMAN / GETTY IMAGES ©

Mercato Centrale

fume, marbled paper, wine, puppets and gourmet foods all make quality souvenirs.

Officina Profumo-Farmaceutica
di Santa Maria Novella   BEAUTY, GIFTS
(Map p70; www.smnovella.it; Via della Scala 16; ☺9.30am-7.30pm) In business since 1612, this perfumery-pharmacy began life when the Dominican friars of Santa Maria Novella began to concoct cures and sweet-smelling unguents using medicinal herbs cultivated in the monastery garden. The shop today sells a wide range of fragrances, skin-care products, ancient herbal remedies and preparations alongside teas, herbal infusions, liqueurs, scented candles, organic olive oil, chocolate, honey and cookies.

& Company   ARTS, CRAFTS
(Map p70; www.andcompanyshop.com; Via Maggio 60r; ☺10.30am-1pm & 3-6.30pm Mon-Sat) This mesmerising Pandora's box of beautiful objects and paper creations is the love child of Florence-born, British-raised calligrapher and graphic designer Betty Soldi and her vintage-loving husband, Matteo Perduca. Together the pair have created an extraordinary boutique showcasing their own customised cards and upcycled homewares alongside work by other designers. Souvenir shopping at its best!

La Bottega Della Frutta   FOOD
(Map p70; Via dei Federighi 31r; ☺8.30am-7.30pm Mon-Sat, closed Aug) Follow the trail of knowing Florentines, past the flower- and veg-laden bicycle parked outside, into this enticing food shop bursting with boutique cheeses, organic fruit and veg, biscuits, chocolates, conserved produce, excellent-value wine et al. Mozzarella oozing raw milk arrives fresh from Eboli in Sicily every Tuesday, and if you're looking to buy olive oil this is the place to taste it. Simply ask Elisabeta or husband Francesco.

Letizia Fiorini   GIFTS, HANDICRAFTS
(Map p70; Via del Parione 60r; ☺10am-7pm Tue-Sat) This charming shop is a one-woman affair – Letizia Fiorini sits at the counter and makes her distinctive puppets by hand in-between assisting customers. You'll find Pulcinella (Punch), Arlecchino the clown, beautiful servant girl Colombina, Doctor Peste (complete with plague mask), cheeky Brighella, swashbuckling Il Capitano and many other characters from traditional Italian puppetry.

DESIGNER OUTLET STORES

Pick up previous-season designer pieces at a snip of the full price at Florence's out-of-town outlet malls.

Barberino Designer Outlet (☑055 84 21 61; www.mcarthurglen.it; Via Meucci, Barberino di Mugello; ☺10am-8pm Mon-Fri, to 9pm Sat & Sun) Previous season's collections by D&G, Prada, Roberto Cavalli, Missoni et al at discounted prices, 40km north of Florence. A shuttle bus (adult/reduced return €15/8, 30 minutes) departs from Piazza della Stazione 44 (in front of Zoppini) two to four times daily. Check seasonal schedules online.

The Mall (☑055 865 77 75; www.themall.it; Via Europa 8, Leccio; ☺10am-8pm summer, to 7pm winter) Shop for last season's Gucci, Ferragamo, Ermenegildo Zegna, Fendi, Valentino et al at this mall, 30km from Florence. Buses (€5, up to eight daily) depart daily from the SITA bus station.

Giulio Giannini e Figlio   HANDICRAFTS
(Map p70; www.giuliogiannini.it; Piazza dei Pitti 37r; ☺10am-7pm Mon-Sat, 11am-6.30pm Sun) This quaint old shopfront has watched Palazzo Pitti turn pink with the evening sun since 1856. One of Florence's oldest artisan families, the Gianninis – bookbinders by trade – make and sell marbled paper, beautifully bound books, stationery and so on. Don't miss the workshop upstairs.

ⓘ Information

EMERGENCY
Police Station (Questura; ☑English-language service 055 497 72 68, 055 4 97 71; questure.poliziadistato.it; Via Zara 2; ☺24hr) Should you have a theft or other unfortunate incident to report, the best time to visit the city's police station is between 9am and 2pm weekdays when the foreign-language service – meaning someone speaks who speaks English – kicks in.

MEDICAL SERVICES
24-Hour Pharmacy (Stazione di Santa Maria Novella; ☺24hrs) There is usually at least one member of staff who speaks English at this pharmacy inside Florence's central train station opens 24 hours.

Dr Stephen Kerr: Medical Service (☑055 28 80 55, 335 8361682; www.dr-kerr.com; Piazza Mercato Nuovo 1; ☺3-5pm Mon-Fri, or

PARKING IN FLORENCE

There is a strict Limited Traffic Zone in Florence's historic centre between 7.30am and 7.30pm Monday to Friday and 7.30am to 6pm Saturday for all nonresidents, monitored by cyclopean cameras positioned at all entry points. The exclusion also applies on Thursday, Friday and Saturday nights from 11pm to 3am late May to mid-September. Motorists staying in hotels within the zone are allowed to drive to their hotel to drop off luggage, but must tell reception their car registration number and the time they were in no-carsland (there's a two-hour window) so that the hotel can inform the authority and organise a permit. If you transgress, a fine of around €150 will be sent to you (or the car-hire company you used). For more information see www.comune.fi.it.

There is free street parking around Piazzale Michelangelo and plenty of car parks costing between €2 and €3 per hour around town, including at Santa Maria Novella train station, by Fortezza da Basso and in the Oltrarno beneath Piazzale di Porta Romana. Find a complete list of car parks on www.firenzeparcheggi.it.

by appointment 9am-3pm Mon-Fri) Resident British doctor.

Hospital (Ospedale di Santa Maria Nuova; 055 2 75 81; Piazza di Santa Maria Nuova 1)

TOURIST INFORMATION

Airport Tourist Office (055 31 58 74; www.firenzeturismo.it; Via del Termine, Aeroporto Vespucci; 9am-7pm Mon-Sat, to 2pm Sun)

Central Tourist Office (055 29 08 32; www.firenzeturismo.it; Via Cavour 1r; 9am-6pm Mon-Sat)

Infopoint Stazione (055 21 22 45; www.firenzeturismo.it; Piazza della Stazione 5; 9am-7pm Mon-Sat, to 2pm Sun)

⊕ Getting There & Around

AIR

Tuscany's main international airport is in Pisa (p121) and offers flights to most major European cities.

Florence Airport (Aeroport Vespucci; 055 306 13 00; www.aeroporto.firenze.it; Via del Termine) Also known as Amerigo Vespucci or Peretola airport, 5km northwest of the city centre; domestic and European flights.

CAR & MOTORCYCLE

Florence is connected by the A1 northwards to Bologna and Milan, and southwards to Rome and Naples. The A11 links Florence with Pistoia, Lucca, Pisa and the coast, but most locals use the FI-PI-LI dual carriageway. Another dual carriageway, the S2, links Florence with Siena.

BICYCLE & SCOOTER

Milleunabici (www.bicifirenze.it; Piazza della Stazione; 1hr/5hr/1 day €2/5/10; 10am-7pm Mar-Oct) Violet coloured bikes to rent in front of Stazione di Santa Maria Novella; leave ID as a deposit.

Florence by Bike (www.florencebybike.com; Via San Zanobi 54r; 1hr/5hr/1 day €3/9/14; 9am-1pm & 3.30-7.30pm Mon-Sat, 9am-5pm Sun summer, closed Sun winter) Top-notch bike shop with bike rental (city, mountain, touring and road bikes), itinerary suggestions and organised bike tours (two-hour photography tours of the city by bike, and day trips to Chianti).

PUBLIC TRANSPORT

Buses and electric minibuses run by public transport company ATAF serve the city. Most buses start/terminate at the bus stops opposite the southeastern exit of Stazione di Santa Maria Novella. Tickets valid for 90 minutes (no return journeys) cost €1.20 (€2 on board) and are sold at kiosks, tobacconists and at the **ATAF ticket & information office** (199 10 42 45, 800 42 45 00; www.ataf.net; Piazza della Stazione, Stazione di Santa Maria Novella; 6.45am-8pm Mon-Sat) inside the main ticketing hall at Santa Maria Novella train station.

A travel pass valid for 1/3/7 days costs €5/12/18. Upon boarding, time-stamp your ticket (punch on board) or risk an on-the-spot €50 fine. One tramline is up and running; more are meant to follow in 2017.

TAXI

Pick one up at the train station or call 055 42 42.

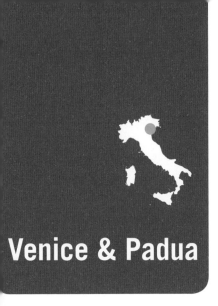

Venice really needs no introduction. This incomparable union of art, architecture and life has been a fabled destination for centuries. Most of the world's most famous writers and artists have visited to admire the mosaics of San Marco, the old masters in the Accademia and the city's maze of calle (lanes) and canals.

Venice & Padua

VENICE

POP 59,000

Imagine the audacity of deciding to build a city on a lagoon. Instead of surrendering to the *acqua alta* (high tide) like reasonable folk might do, Venetians flooded the world with vivid paintings, baroque music, modern opera, spice-route cuisine, bohemian-chic fashions and a Grand Canal's worth of *spritz,* the city's signature *prosecco* and Aperol cocktail.

Today cutting-edge architects and billionaire benefactors are spicing up the art scene, musicians are rocking 18th-century instruments and backstreet *osterie* (taverns) are winning a Slow Food following.

Like a cat with nine lives, Venice has miraculously survived over 1200 years of war, plague and invasion, but it now faces its greatest threat: rising sea levels. This remains the biggest challenge facing the city, with rises of between 14cm and 80cm predicted by 2100.

◎ Sights

Basilica di San Marco   BASILICA
(St Mark's Basilica; ☑ 041 270 83 11; www.basilica sanmarco.it; Piazza San Marco; ⊙ 9.45am-5pm Mon-Sat, 2-5pm Sun summer, to 4pm Sun winter; ⊠ San Marco) In AD 828, wily Venetian merchants allegedly smuggled St Mark's corpse out of Egypt in a barrel of pork fat to avoid inspection by Muslim customs authorities. Venice built a golden basilica around its stolen saint, taking 800 years to complete.

The brick basilica is clad in patchworks of marbles and reliefs from Syria, Egypt and Palestine – priceless trophies from Crusades conquests and battles with Genoa. Inside, the glittering mosaics of the dome vie for attention with the Pala d'Oro, studded with 2000 emeralds, amethysts, sapphires, rubies, pearls and other gemstones.

Palazzo Ducale   MUSEUM
(Ducal Palace; ☑ 041 271 59 11; www.palazzoducale. visitmuve.it; Piazzetta San Marco 52; incl Museo Correr adult/reduced €18/11; ⊙ 8.30am-7pm summer, to 5.30pm winter; ⊠ San Zaccaria) Don't be fooled by the genteel Gothic elegance: under its lacy pink facade and rosy Veronese ceilings, the Ducal Palace – the seat of Venice's government for nearly seven centuries – flexes serious political muscle. The white Istrian stone and Veronese pink marble palace caps a graceful colonnade with medieval capitals depicting key Venetian guilds. Today the council chambers are stuffed with masterpieces, while the ancient prison cells and interrogation rooms display its more grisly past.

Campanile   TOWER
(Bell Tower; www.basilicasanmarco.it; Piazza San Marco; admission €8; ⊙ 9am-9pm summer, to 7pm spring & autumn, 9.30am-3.45pm winter; ⊠ San Marco) The basilica's 99m-tall tower has been rebuilt twice since its initial construction in AD 888, and Galileo Galilei found it handy

Venice

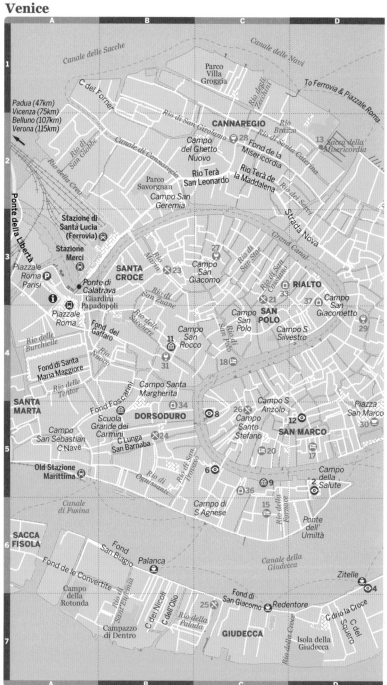

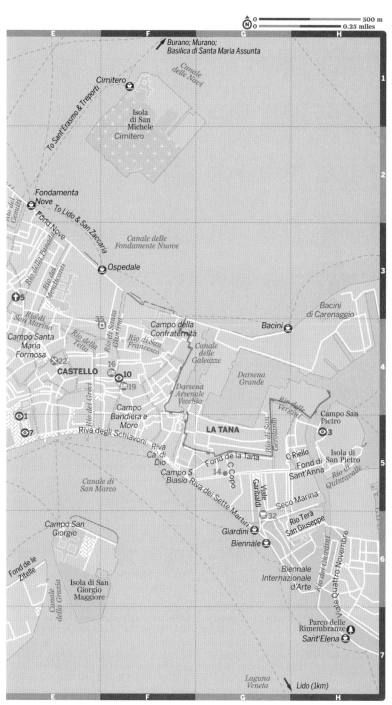

Burano; Murano;
Basilica di Santa Maria Assunta

Canale
delle Navi

Cimitero

Isola
di San
Michele
Cimitero

To Sant'Erasmo & Treporti

Fondamenta
Nove

Fond Nove

To Lido & San Zaccaria

Canale delle
Fondamente Nuove

Ospedale

5

35

Campo della
Confraternità

Bacini
di Carenaggio

Bacini

Rio di
San Marina

Campo Santa
Maria
Formosa

CASTELLO

22

16

10

19

Canale
delle
Galeazze

Darsena
Grande

Darsena
Arsenale
Vecchio

Campo
Bandiera e
Moro
Riva degli Schiavoni

Riva
Ca' di
Dio

LA TANA

Campo San
Pietro

3

1

7

Canale di
San Marco

Fond de la Tana

14 C. Copo

Campo S
Biasio Riva dei Sette Martiri

C Riello

Fond di
Sant'Anna

Isola di
San Pietro

Rio di
Quintavalle

Campo San
Giorgio

Isola di San
Giorgio
Maggiore

Fond de le
Zitelle

Canale
della Grazia

Viale
Garibaldi

Seco Marina

Giardini

Biennale

32

Rio Tera
San Giuseppe

Viale Quattro Novembre

Biennale
Internazionale
d'Arte

Parco delle
Rimembranze

Sant'Elena

7

Laguna
Veneta

Lido (1km)

0   500 m
0   0.25 miles

79

Venice

for testing his telescope in 1609. Critics called Bartolomeo Bon's 16th-century tower redesign ungainly, but when this version suddenly collapsed in 1902, Venetians rebuilt the tower as it was, brick by brick.

Teatro La Fenice   THEATRE
(☏041 78 66 75; www.teatrolafenice.it; Campo San Fantin 1965; theatre visits adult/reduced €9/6.50, opera tickets from €66; ☺tours 9.30am-6pm; ☻Santa Maria del Giglio) Rossini and Bellini staged operas here, Verdi premiered *Rigoletto* and *La Traviata*, and international greats Stravinsky, Prokofiev and Britten composed for the house, making La Fenice the envy of Europe. From January to July and September to October, opera season is in full swing. Tours are also possible with advance booking.

Palazzo Grassi   MUSEUM
(☏box office 199 13 91 39, 041 523 16 80; www.palazzograssi.it; Campo San Samuele 3231; adult/reduced €15/10; ☺10am-7pm Wed-Mon mid-Apr–Nov; ☻San Samuele) Grand Canal gondola riders gasp at the first glimpse of massive sculptures by contemporary artists like Thomas Houseago docked in front of Giorgio Masari's neoclassical palace. French billionaire François Pinault's provocative art collection overflows from Palazzo

Grassi, while clever curation and art-star name-dropping are the hallmarks of rotating temporary exhibits. Despite the glamour, Tadao Ando's creatively repurposed interior architecture steals the show.

Gallerie dell'Accademia   GALLERY
(☏041 520 03 45; www.gallerieaccademia.org; Campo della Carità 1050; adult/reduced €11/8 plus supplement during special exhibitions, first Sun of the month free; ☺8.15am-2pm Mon, to 7.15pm Tue-Sun; ☻Accademia) Hardly academic, these galleries contain more murderous intrigue, forbidden romance and shameless politicking than the most outrageous Venetian parties. The former Santa Maria della Carità convent complex maintained its serene composure for centuries, but ever since Napoleon installed his haul of Venetian art trophies in 1807, there's been nonstop visual drama inside these walls, with Carpaccio, Tintoretto, Titian and Veronese jostling for space.

Peggy Guggenheim Collection   MUSEUM
(☏041 240 54 11; www.guggenheim-venice.it; Palazzo Venier dei Leoni 704; adult/reduced €15/9; ☺10am-6pm Wed-Mon; ☻Accademia) After losing her father on the *Titanic,* heiress Peggy Guggenheim became one of the great collectors of the 20th century. Her palatial canalside home, Palazzo Venier dei Leoni, showcases her stock

pile of surrealist, futurist and abstract expressionist art with works by up to 200 artists, including her ex-husband Max Ernst, Jackson Pollock (among her many rumoured lovers), Picasso and Salvador Dalí.

Basilica di Santa Maria della Salute
BASILICA

(La Salute; ☑ 041 241 10 18; www.seminariovenezia.it; Campo della Salute 1b; admission free, sacristy adult/reduced €3/1.50; ⊙ 9am-noon & 3-5.30pm; ☀ Salute) Commissioned by Venice's plague survivors as thanks for salvation, Baldassare Longhena's uplifting design is an engineering feat that defies logic; in fact, the church is said to have mystical curative properties. Titian eluded the plague until age 90, leaving a legacy of masterpieces now in Salute's sacristy.

Scuola Grande di San Rocco
MUSEUM

(☑ 041 523 48 64; www.scuolagrandesanrocco.it; Campo San Rocco 3052, San Polo; adult/reduced €10/8; ⊙ 9.30am-5.30pm, Tesoro to 5.15pm; ☀ San Tomà) Everyone wanted the commission to paint this building dedicated to the patron saint of the plague-stricken, so Tintoretto cheated: instead of producing sketches like rival Veronese, he gifted a splendid ceiling panel of patron St Roch, knowing it couldn't be refused or matched by other artists. The artist documents Mary's life story in the assembly hall, and both Old and New Testament scenes in the Sala Grande Superiore upstairs.

Chiesa di Santa Maria dei Miracoli
CHURCH

(Campo dei Miracoli 6074; admission €2.50; ⊙ 10am-5pm Mon-Sat; ☀ Fondamenta Nuove) When Nicolò di Pietro's Madonna icon started miraculously weeping in its outdoor shrine around 1480, crowd control became impossible. With pooled resources and marble scavenged from San Marco slag heaps, neighbours built this chapel (1481–89) to house the painting. Pietro and Tullio Lombardo's design dropped grandiose Gothic in favour of human-scale harmonies, introducing Renaissance architecture to Venice.

Scuola di San Giorgio degli Schiavoni
CHURCH

(☑ 041 522 88 28; Calle dei Furlani 3259a; adult/reduced €5/3; ⊙ 2.45-6pm Mon, 9.15am-1pm & 2.45-6pm Tue-Sat, 9.15am-1pm Sun; ☀ Pietà) Venice's cosmopolitan nature is evident in Castello, where Turkish merchants, Armenian clerics and Balkan and Slavic labourers were considered essential to Venetian commerce and society. This 15th-century religious confraternity headquarters is dedicated to favourite

Slavic saints George, Tryphone and Jerome of Dalmatia, whose lives are captured with precision and glowing, early-Renaissance grace by 15th-century master Vittore Carpaccio.

Casa dei Tre Oci
CULTURAL CENTRE

(☑ 041 241 23 32; www.treoci.org; Fondamente de la Croce 43; exhibits €5; ⊙ 10am-6pm Wed-Mon; ☀ Zitelle) FREE Acquired by the Fondazione di Venezia in 2000, this fanciful neo-Gothic house was once the home of early-20th-century artist and photographer Mario de Maria, who conceived its distinctive brick facade with its three arched windows (its namesake 'eyes') in 1910. Now it hosts his photographic archive and fantastic Italian and international exhibitions of contemporary art and photography. The views of San Marco and the Punta della Dogana alone are worth the visit.

Basilica di Santa Maria Assunta
CHURCH

(☑ 041 73 01 19; Piazza Torcello; adult/reduced €5/4; ⊙ 10.30am-6pm summer, 10am-5pm winter; ☀ Torcello) Life choices are presented in no uncertain terms in the dazzling 12th-century mosaics of Santa Maria Assunta. Look ahead to an afterlife amid saints and a beatific Madonna, or turn your back on her and face the wrath of the devil gloating over lost souls in an extraordinary *Last Judgment* panel. The cathedral is the Lagoon's oldest Byzantine-Romanesque monument and after lengthy restorations you can once again enjoy the heavenly views from the *campanile*.

Murano
ISLAND

(☀ 4.1, 4.2) Murano has been the home of Venetian glassmaking since the 13th century. Tour a factory for a behind-the-scenes look at production or visit the Museo del Vetro

---

❶ OUTSMARTING ACCADEMIA QUEUES

To skip Accademia ticket-booth queues, book ahead by calling ☑ 041 520 03 45 (booking fee €1). Otherwise, queues tend to be shorter in the afternoon. But don't wait too long: the last entry to the Accademia is 45 minutes before closing, and proper visits take at least 90 minutes.

Leave any large items at the baggage depot (€1 refundable). Also available at the baggage depot is an audio guide (€6) that is mostly descriptive and largely unnecessary – it's better to avoid the wait and just follow the explanatory wall tags.

Masked Carnevale reveller

(Glass Museum; ☏ 041 527 47 18; www.museovetro. visitmuve.it; Fondamenta Giustinian 8; adult/reduced €10/7.50; ☻10am-6pm Apr-Oct, to 5pm Nov-Mar; ⛴Museo) near the Museo *vaporetto* (water bus) stop. Note that at the time of writing the museum was undergoing a major overhaul.

Burano   ISLAND
(⛴12) Burano, with its cheery pastel-coloured houses, is renowned for its hand-made lace. These days, however, much of the lace sold in local shops is imported.

🏃 Activities & Tours

A gondola ride (☏ 041 528 50 75; www.gondola venezia.it) gives glimpses into *palazzi* court-yards and hidden canals otherwise unseen on foot. Official daytime rates are €80 for 40 minutes (six passengers maximum), and it's €100 between 7pm and 8am, not including songs (negotiated separately) or tips. Additional time is charged in 20-minute increments (day/night €40/50). Gondolas cluster at *stazi* (stops) along the Grand Canal, and at the train station, the Rialto and near monuments, but you can also book a pick-up by calling the main number.

Cheaper shared gondola rides are available through Tu.Ri.Ve (www.turive.it), either by booking online or through the tourist office.

Row Venice   ROWING
(☏ 347 7250637; rowvenice.org; 90min lessons 1-2 people €80, 4 people €120) The next best thing to walking on water: rowing a traditional *batellina coda di gambero* (shrimp-tailed boat) standing up like gondoliers. Tours must be booked and start at the gate of the Sacca Misericordia boat marina at the end of Fonda-menta Gasparo Contarini in Cannaregio.

Venice Photo Walk   WALKING TOUR
(☏ 041 963 73 74; www.msecchi.com; 2/3/6 hr walk-ing tours up to 4 people €210/300/600) Through-out San Marco you'll be tripping over smartphone-touting tourists waving selfie sticks. Everyone, it seems, wants to capture the perfect Venetian scene. Getty photojour-nalist Marco Secchi will show you how.

VeniceArtFactory   CULTURAL TOUR
(☏ 349 779 93 85, 328 658 38 71; www.veniceart factory.org; Via Garibaldi 1794; 2-person tours €180, additional adult/student €40/20; ⛴Arsenale) VeniceArtFactory's Studio Tours allow you to sit down to breakfast or share an *aperitivo* with painters, sculptors and engravers in their studios and homes and ask them what it's like to be an artist in the most artful city in the world.

✨ Festivals & Events

Carnevale   CARNIVAL
(www.carnevale.venezia.it) Masquerade mad-ness stretches over two weeks in February before Lent. Tickets to masked balls start at €140, but there's a free-flowing wine foun-tain to commence Carnevale, public cos-tume parties in every square and a Grand Canal flotilla marking the end of festivities.

La Biennale di Venezia CULTURAL

(www.labiennale.org) In odd years the Art Biennale runs from June to October, while in even years the Architecture Biennale runs from September to November. The main venues are Giardini Pubblici pavilions and the Arsenale. Every summer, the Biennale hosts avant-garde dance, theatre, cinema and music programs throughout the city.

🛏 Sleeping

B&B Corte Vecchia B&B €

(☎041 822 12 33; www.cortevecchia.net; Rio Terà San Vio 462; s €60-100, d €100-130; ❄ 🌐; 🚤 Accademia) Corte Vecchia is a stylish steal, run by young architects Antonella and Mauro and a stone's throw from Peggy Guggenheim and Accademia. Choose from a snug single with en suite, or two good-sized doubles: one with en suite, the other with an external private bathroom. All are simple yet understatedly cool, with contemporary and vintage objects, and a tranquil, shared lounge.

B&B San Marco B&B €

(☎041 522 75 89; www.realvenice.it/smarco; Fondamente San Giorgio 3385l; d €70-135; ❄ 🌐; 🚤 Pietà, Arsenale) One of the few genuine B&Bs in Venice. Alice and Marco welcome you warmly to their home overlooking Carpaccio's frescoed Scuola di San Giorgio Schiavoni. The 3rd-floor apartment (there is no elevator), with its parquet floors and large, bright windows, is furnished with family antiques and offers views over the terracotta rooftops and canals. Marco and Alice live upstairs, so they're always on hand with great recommendations.

Hotel Flora HOTEL €€

(☎041 520 58 44; www.hotelflora.it; Calle Bergamaschi 2283a; d €105-365; ❄ 🌐 👪; 🚤 Santa Maria del Giglio) Down a lane from glitzy Calle Larga XXII Marzo, this ivy-covered retreat quietly outclasses brash designer neighbours with its delightful tea room, breakfasts around the garden fountain and gym offering shiatsu massage. Guest rooms feature antique mirrors, hand-carved beds, and tiled en suite baths with apothecary-style amenities. Strollers and kids' teatime complimentary; babysitting available.

Hotel Sant'Antonin BOUTIQUE HOTEL €€

(☎041 523 16 21; www.hotelsantantonin.com; Fondamenta dei Furlani 3299; d €100-280; ❄ 🌐 👪; 🚤 San Zaccaria) Enjoy the patrician pleasures of a wealthy Greek merchant at this 16th-century *palazzo* perched on a canal near the Greek church. Grand proportions make for light, spacious rooms with cool terrazzo floors, balconies, frescoed ceilings and impressive baroque furnishings. Come breakfast you can trip down the stone staircase and out into one of the largest private gardens in Venice.

Novecento BOUTIQUE HOTEL €€€

(☎041 241 37 65; www.novecento.biz; Calle del Dose 2683/84; d €160-340; ❄ 🌐; 🚤 Santa Maria del Giglio) Sporting a boho-chic look, the Novocento is a real charmer. Its nine individually designed rooms ooze style with Turkish kilim pillows, Fortuny draperies and 19th-century carved bedsteads. Outside, its garden is a lovely spot to linger over breakfast. Want more? You can go for a massage at sister property Hotel Flora, take a course in landscape drawing, or mingle with creative fellow travellers around the honesty bar.

Hotel Palazzo Barbarigo DESIGN HOTEL €€€

(☎041 740 172; www.palazzobarbarigo.com; Grand Canal 2765, San Polo; d €240-440; ❄ 🌐; 🚤 San Tomà) Brooding, chic and seductive, Barbarigo delivers 18 plush guest rooms combining modern elegance and masquerade intrigue – think contemporary furniture, sumptuous velvets, feathered lamps and the occasional fainting couch. Whether you opt for junior suites overlooking the Grand Canal (get triple-windowed Room 10) or standard rooms overlooking Rio di San Polo, you can indulge in sleek bathrooms, positively royal breakfasts and smart, attentive service.

🍴 Eating

Osteria Ruga di Jaffa OSTERIA €

(Ruga Giuffa 4864; meals €20-25; ⏰8am-11pm) Hiding in plain sight on the busy Ruga Giuffa is this excellent *osteria* (casual tavern). You should be able to spot it by the gondoliers packing out the tables at lunchtime. They may not appreciate the vase of blooming hydrangeas on the bar or the arty Murano wall lamps, but they thoroughly approve of the select menu of housemade pastas and succulent over-roast pork soaked in its own savoury juices.

Ristorante La Bitta RISTORANTE €€

(☎041 523 05 31; Calle Lunga San Barnaba 2753a; meals €35-40; ⏰6.45-10.45pm Mon-Sat; 🚤 Ca' Rezzonico) Recalling a cosy bistro, La Bitta keeps punters purring with hearty rustic fare made using the freshest ingredients – the fact that the kitchen has no freezer ensures this. Scan the daily menu for mouthwatering, seasonal options like tagliatelle with artichoke thistle and gorgonzola or juicy pork *salsiccette* (small sausages) served with *verze* (local cabbage) and warming polenta. Reservations essential. Cash only.

Antiche Carampane
VENETIAN €€
(☑ 041 524 01 65; www.antichecarampane.com; Rio Terà delle Carampane 1911, San Polo; meals €30-45; ☺ 12.45-2.30pm & 7.30-10.30pm Tue-Sat; ⚲ San Stae) Hidden in the once-shady lanes behind Ponte delle Tette, this culinary indulgence is a trick to find. Once you do, say goodbye to soggy lasagne and hello to a market-driven menu of silky *crudi* (raw fish or seafood), surprisingly light *fritto misto* (fried seafood) and prawn salad with seasonal vegetables.

Osteria Trefanti
VENETIAN €€
(☑ 041 520 17 89; www.osteriatrefanti.it; Fondamenta Garzotti 888, Santa Croce; meals €40; ☺ noon-2.30pm & 7-10.30pm Tue-Sat, noon-2.45pm Sun; 🖥; ⚲ Riva de Biasio) 🌿 La Serenissima's spice trade lives on at simple, elegant Trefanti, where a vibrant dish of marinated prawns, hazelnuts, berries and caramel might get an intriguing kick from garam masala. Furnished with old pews and recycled copper lamps it has a small, beautifully curated selection of local and organic wines.

Trattoria e Bacaro
Da Fiore
VENETIAN, CICHETI €€€
(☑ 041 523 53 10; www.dafiore.it; Calle delle Botteghe 3461; meals €45-80, cicheti €10-15; ☺ 12.30-2.30pm & 7.30-10.30pm Tue-Sat; ⚲ San Samuele) Possibly the best bang for your buck in San Marco, this elegant trattoria with its rustic-chic decor serves superlative Venetian dishes composed of carefully selected seasonal ingredients from small Veneto producers. Next door, the

cicheti (bar snacks) counter serves excellent *cicheti* at more democratic prices.

Trattoria Altanella
VENETIAN €€€
(☑ 041 522 77 80; Calle delle Erbe 268; meals €35-45; ☺ noon-2.30pm & 7-10.30pm Tue-Sat; ⚲ Palanca) In 1920 fisherman Nane Stradella and his wife, Irma, opened a trattoria overlooking the Rio di Ponte Longo. Their fine Venetian cooking was so successful he soon gave up fishing and the restaurant now sustains a fourth generation of family cooks. Inside, the vintage interior is hung with artworks, reflecting the restaurant's popularity with artists, poets and writers, while outside a flower-fringed balcony hangs over the canal.

 ## Drinking

Bacarando
BAR
(☑ 041 523 82 80; Corte dell'Orso 5495; ☺ 9.30am-midnight) If you've managed to find this warm, wood-panelled bar in the warren of streets off San Bartolomeo, toast yourself with a radical rum cocktail (this place has over 150 different labels) and order a huge burger or a plate of heaped *cicheti*. Thanks to its clubby vibe and a lively program of cultural events and live music, it's popular with a hip young crowd.

Estro
WINE BAR
(www.estrovenezia.com; Dorsoduro 3778; ☺ 11am-midnight Wed-Mon, kitchen closes 10pm) New entry Estro is anything you want it to be: wine and charcuterie bar, *aperitivo* pit stop, or degustation restaurant. The 500 *vini* (wines) – many of them natural-process wines – are chosen by young-gun sibling owners Alberto and Dario, whose passion for quality extends to the grub, from *cicheti*

EATING & DRINKING LIKE A VENETIAN

Why drink alone? **Venice Urban Adventures** (☑ 348 980 85 66; www.venice urbanadventures.com; cicheti tours €77; ☺ tours 11.30am & 5.30pm Mon-Sat) offers intimate tours of happy-hour hotspots led by knowledgeable, enthusiastic, English-speaking local foodies. Tours have up to 12 participants and cover *ombre* (wine by the glass) and *cicheti* (bar snacks) in five (yes, five) *bacari* (wine bars), and a tipsy Rialto gondola ride (weather permitting). Tours depart from Campo della Maddalena in Cannaregio and end at Ponte di Rialto (Rialto Bridge).

If you want to learn to cook like an Italian mama or eat like a Venetian gondolier look no further than **Cook in Venice** (www.cookinvenice.com; tours €35 to €60, courses €140 to €225), Monica and Arianna's wonderful cookery classes and food tours. These two Venetian cooks are a tour de force: warmly welcoming, engaging teachers and passionate connoisseurs of Venetian food and wine. Whipping up *polpettas* or *zabaglione* in Arianna's country home is a truly memorable experience, while Monica's food tours have earned high praise from Katie Caldesi, Alex Polizzi and numerous well-fed chefs!

topped with house-made *porchetta* (roast pork), to a burger made with asiago cheese and house-made ketchup and mayonnaise.

Al Prosecco
WINE BAR

(✒041 524 02 22; www.alprosecco.com; Campo San Giacomo dell'Orio, Santa Croce 1503; ◷10am-8pm; ⛴San Stae) ✐ The urge to toast sunsets in Venice's loveliest *campo* is only natural – and so is the wine at Al Prosecco. This forward-thinking bar specialises in *vini naturi* (natural-process wines) – organic, biodynamic, wild yeast fermented – from enlightened Italian winemakers like Cinque Campi and Azienda Agricola Barichel. So order a glass of unfiltered 'cloudy' prosecco and toast the good things in life

Al Timon
WINE BAR

(✒041 524 60 66; Fondamenta degli Ormesini 2754; ◷11am-1am Thu-Tue & 6pm-1am Wed; ⛴San Marcuola) Find a spot on the boat moored out front along the canal and watch the motley parade of drinkers and dreamers arrive for seafood *crostini* (open-face sandwiches) and quality organic and DOC wines by the *ombra* (half-glass of wine) or carafe. Folk singers play sets canalside when the weather obliges; when it's cold, regulars scoot over to make room for newcomers at indoor tables.

Caffè Florian
CAFE

See p23

La Serra dei Giardini
CAFE

(✒041 296 03 60; www.serradeigiardini.org; Viale Giuseppe Garibaldi 1254; snacks €4-15; ◷10am-9.30pm summer, 11am-8pm Mon-Thu & 10am-9pm Fri & Sat winter; ☎⛗; ⛴Giardini) Order a herbal tisane or the signature pear Bellini and sit back amid the hothouse flowers in Napoleon's fabulous greenhouse. Cathedral-like windows look out onto the tranquil greenery of the public gardens, while upstairs workshops in painting and gardening are hosted on the suspended mezzanine. Light snacks and cakes are also available alongside unique microbrews and Lurisia sodas flavoured with Slow Food Presidia products.

🛍 Shopping

Venice abounds with unique finds at surprisingly reasonable prices, handmade by artisans in Murano and backstreet studios.

Cárte
HANDICRAFTS

(✒320 0248776; www.cartevenezia.it; Calle dei Cristi 1731, San Polo; ◷11am-5.30pm; ⛴Rialto-Mercato) Venice's shimmering lagoon echoes in marbled-paper earrings and artist's portfolios, thanks to the steady hands and restless imagination of *carta marmorizzata* (marbled-paper) *maestra* Rosanna Corrò. After years restoring ancient Venetian books, Rosanna began creating her original, bookish beauties: tubular statement necklaces, op-art jewellery boxes, one-of-a-kind contemporary handbags, even wedding albums.

Danghyra
CERAMICS

(✒041 522 41 95; www.danghyra.com; Calle de le Botteghe 3220; ◷10am-1pm & 3-7pm Tue-Sun; ⛴Ca' Rezzonico) Spare white bisque cups seem perfect for a Zen tea ceremony, but look inside: that iridescent lilac glaze is pure Carnevale. Danghyra's striking ceramics are hand-thrown in Venice with a magic touch – her platinum-glazed bowls make the simplest pasta dish appear fit for a modern doge.

Marina e Susanna Sent
GLASS

(✒041 520 81 36; www.marinaesusannasent.com; Campo San Vio 669; ◷10am-1pm & 1.30-6.30pm; ⛴Accademia) Wearable waterfalls and un-poppable soap-bubble necklaces are Venice style signatures, thanks to the Murano-born Sent sisters. Defying centuries-old beliefs that women can't handle molten glass, their minimalist art-glass statement jewellery is featured in museum shops worldwide, from Palazzo Grassi to MoMA. See new collections at this flagship, their Murano studio, or the San Marco branch (at Ponte San Moise 2090).

Pied à Terre
SHOES

(✒041 528 55 13; www.piedaterre-venice.com; Sotoportego degli Oresi 60, San Polo; ◷10am-12.30pm & 2.30-7.30pm; ⛴Rialto) Rialto courtesans and their 30cm-high heels are long gone, but Venetian slippers remain stylish. Pied à Terre's colourful *furlane* (slippers) are hand-crafted with recycled bicycle-tyre treads, ideal for finding your footing on a gondola. Choose from velvet, brocade or raw silk in vibrant shades of lemon and ruby, with optional piping. Don't see your size? Shoes can be custom made and shipped.

Fabricharte
CRAFTS

(✒041 200 67 43; www.fabricharte.org; Calle del Cafetier 6477/Z; ◷11am-7pm Mon-Sat; ⛴Fondamente Nove) Stacks of hand-bound books, picture frames, trays and keepsake boxes all covered in delightful, hand-stamped papers make the the window of Andreatta Andrea's workshop look like Christmas. He apprenticed at the legendary Piazzesi and now offers a unique service in Venice: bring him any well-loved book and he can rebind it for you in any of the available Raimondini papers in a day or two. He also fashions gift-worthy sketch pads and composition books.

❶ Information

EMERGENCY

For an ambulance, call ☑118. Call ☑112 or ☑113 for the police.

Police Headquarters (☑ 041 271 55 11; Santa Croce 500) San Marco's head police station is off the beaten track in the ex-convent of Santa Chiara, just beyond Piazzale Roma.

MEDICAL SERVICES

Information on rotating late-night pharmacies is posted in pharmacy windows and listed in the free magazine *Un Ospite di Venezia*, available at the tourist office.

Guardia Medica (☑ 041 238 56 48) This service of night-time call-out doctors in Venice operates from 8pm to 8am on weekdays and from 10am the day before a holiday (including Sunday) until 8am the day after.

Ospedale Civile (☑ 041 529 41 11; Campo SS Giovanni e Paolo 6777; 🚢 Ospedale) Venice's main hospital; for emergency care and dental treatment.

TOURIST INFORMATION

Airport Tourist Office (☑ 041 529 87 11; www.turismovenezia.it; Arrivals Hall, Marco Polo Airport; ⏰ 8.30am-7.30pm)

❶ Getting There & Away

CAR & MOTORCYCLE

The congested Trieste–Turin A4 passes through Mestre. From Mestre, take the Venice exit. From the south, take the A13 from Bologna, which connects with the A4 at Padua.

Once over the Ponte della Libertà bridge from Mestre, cars must be left at the car park at Piazzale Roma or Tronchetto; expect to pay €21 or more for every 24 hours. Parking stations in Mestre are cheaper. Car ferry 17 transports vehicles from Tronchetto to the Lido.

Avis, Europcar and Hertz all have car rental offices on Piazzale Roma and at Marco Polo airport. Several companies operate in or near Mestre train station, too.

Interparking (Tronchetto Car Park; ☑ 041 520 75 55; www.veniceparking.it; Isola del Tronchetto; per 2/3-5/5-24hr €3/5/21; ⏰ 24hr) Has 3957 spaces; the largest lot with the cheapest 24-hour rate. *Vaporetti* connect directly with Piazza San Marco, while the People Mover provides connections to Piazzale Roma and the cruise terminal.

❶ Getting Around

VAPORETTO

The city's main mode of public transport is *vaporetto* – Venice's distinctive water bus. Tickets can be purchased from the HelloVenezia ticket booths at most landing stations. You can also buy tickets when boarding; you may be charged double with luggage, though this is not always enforced.

Instead of spending €7 for a one-way ticket, consider a Travel Card, which is a timed pass for unlimited travel (beginning at first validation). Passes for 24/48/72 hours cost €20/30/40. A week pass costs €60.

WATER TAXIS

The standard **water taxi** (Consorzio Motoscafi Venezia; 24hr ☑ 041 522 23 03, Marco Polo airport desk ☑ 041 541 50 84; www.motoscafi venezia.it) between Marco Polo airport and Venice costs €110 for a private taxi and €25 per person for a shared taxi with up to 10 passengers. Elsewhere in Venice, official taxi rates start at €15 plus €2 per minute and €6 extra if they're called to your hotel. Night trips, extra luggage and large groups cost more. Prices are metered or negotiated in advance.

PADUA

POP 209,700

Though under an hour from Venice, Padua seems a world away with its medieval marketplaces, fascist-era facades and hip student population. As a medieval city-state home to Italy's second-oldest university, Padua challenged both Venice and Verona for regional hegemony. An extraordinary series of fresco cycles recalls this golden age – including Giotto's remarkable Cappella degli Scrovegni.

◉ Sights

Cappella degli Scrovegni   CHURCH
(See p22; Scrovegni Chapel; ☑ 049 201 00 20; www.cappelladegliscrovegni.it; Piazza Eremitani 8; adult/reduced €13/6, night ticket €8/6; ⏰ 9am-7pm, also 7-10pm various periods through year) Padua's version of the Sistine Chapel, the Cappella degli Scrovegni houses one of Italy's great Renaissance masterpieces – a striking cycle of Giotto frescoes. Giotto ended the Dark Ages with these paintings (1303–05), whose humanistic depictions showed biblical figures as characters in recognisable settings.

Musei Civici agli Eremitani   MUSEUM
(☑ 049 820 45 51; Piazza Eremitani 8; adult/reduced €10/8; ⏰ 9am-7pm Tue-Sun) Among the showstoppers here is a crucifix by Giotto, showing Mary wringing her hands as Jesus' blood

drips into the empty eye sockets of a human skull. Mary also appears in a series of dazzling paintings by 14th-century artist Guariento di Arpo, executed for the private chapel of Padua's powerful Carraresi (da Carrara) family.

Palazzo Zuckermann GALLERY
(☑049 820 56 64; Corso di Garibaldi 33; adult/reduced €10/8; ⊙10am-7pm Tue-Sun) The ground and 1st floors of the early-20th-century Palazzo Zuckermann are home to the Museo d'Arti Applicate e Decorative, whose eclectic assortment of decorative and applied arts spans several centuries of flatware, furniture, fashion and jewellery.

Palazzo del Bò HISTORIC BUILDING
See p22

Palazzo della Ragione HISTORIC BUILDING
(☑049 820 50 06; Piazza delle Erbe; adult/reduced €4/2; ⊙9am-7pm Tue-Sun, to 6pm Nov-Jan) Ancient Padua can be glimpsed in elegant twin squares separated by the Gothic Palazzo della Ragione, the city's tribunal dating from 1218. Inside Il Salone (the Great Hall), frescoes by Giotto acolytes Giusto de' Menabuoi and Nicolò Miretto depict the months, seasons, saints, animals and noteworthy Paduans. The enormous 15th-century wooden horse at the western end of the hall was modelled on Donatello's majestic bronze *Gattamelata*, which still stands in Piazza del Santo. At the other end of the hall is a contemporary version of Foucault's *Pendulum*.

Duomo CATHEDRAL
(☑049 65 69 14; Piazza del Duomo; baptistry €3; ⊙7.30am-noon & 4-7.30pm Mon-Sat, 8am-1pm & 4-8.45pm Sun & holidays, baptistry 10am-6pm) Built from a much-altered design of Michelangelo's, the whitewashed symmetry of Padua's cathedral is a far cry from its rival in Piazza San Marco. Pop in quickly for Giuliano Vangi's contemporary chancel crucifix and sculptures before taking in the adjoining 13th-century baptistry, a Romanesque gem frescoed with luminous biblical scenes by Giusto de' Menabuoi. Hundreds of male and female saints congregate in the cupola, posed as though for a school photo, exchanging glances and stealing looks at the Madonna.

Basilica di Sant'Antonio CHURCH
See p22

Oratorio di San Giorgio & Scoletta del Santo CHURCH
(☑049 822 56 52; Piazza del Santo; adult/reduced €5/4; ⊙9am-12.30pm & 2.30-7pm Apr-Sep, to 5pm

Orto Botanico
LYSVIK PHOTOS / SHUTTERSTOCK ©

Oct-Mar) Anywhere else the fresco cycle of the Oratorio di San Giorgio and the paintings in the Scoletta del Santo would be considered highlights, but in Padua they must contend with Giotto's Scrovegni brilliance. This means you'll have Altichiero da Zevio and Jacopo Avanzi's jewel-like, 14th-century frescoes of St George, St Lucy and St Catherine all to yourself, while upstairs in the *scoletta* (confraternity house), Titian paintings are viewed in rare tranquillity.

Orto Botanico GARDENS
(☑049 201 02 22; www.ortobotanicopd.it; Via dell'Orto Botanico 15; adult/reduced €10/8; ⊙9am-7pm daily Apr & May, 9am-7pm Tue-Sun Jun-Sep, to 6pm Tue-Sun Oct, to 5pm Tue-Sun Nov-Mar; ☎♿) Planted in 1545 by Padua University's medical faculty to study the medicinal properties of rare plants, Padua's World Heritage–listed Orto Botanico served as a clandestine Resistance meeting headquarters in WWII. The oldest tree is nicknamed 'Goethe's palm'; planted in 1585, it was mentioned by the great German writer in his *Voyage in Italy*.

🛌 Sleeping

Ostello Città di Padova HOSTEL €
(☑049 875 22 19; www.ostellopadova.it; Via dei Aleardi 30; dm €19-23, d €46, without bathroom €40; ⊙reception 7.15-9.30am & 3.30-11.30pm; ☎) A central hostel with decent four- and six-bed dorm rooms on a quiet side street. There's an 11.30pm curfew, except when

Padua

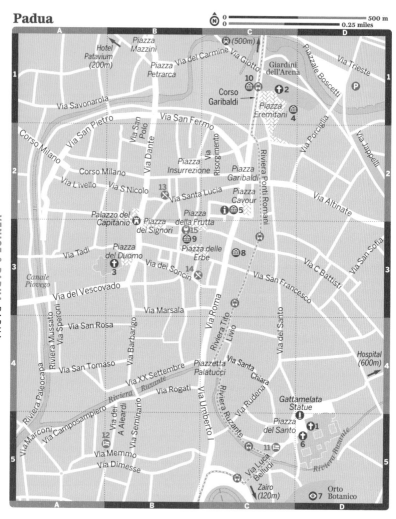

there are special events, and guests must check out by 9.30am. Take bus 12 or 18, or the tram from the train station.

Belludi37
BOUTIQUE HOTEL €€
(☑049 66 56 33; www.belludi37.it; Via Luca Belludi 37; s €80, d €140-180; ❋🤝) Graced with Flos bedside lamps and replica Danish chairs, the neutrally toned rooms at Belludi37 feature high ceilings, queen-sized beds and free minibar. Six new rooms also deliver svelte bathrooms. Extra perks include a central location and staff always on hand with suggestions for biking routes and walking tours.

Hotel Patavium
HOTEL €€
(☑049 72 36 98; www.hotelpatavium.it; Via B Pellegrino 106; s €60-120, d €75-140; ❋🤝) Smart, carpeted rooms with wide beds, flat-screen TVs and modern bathrooms define Hotel Patavium, a quick walk northwest of the city centre. Suites come with Jacuzzis, while the breakfast room has candlesticks, chandeliers and a corner lounge with a communal TV.

Padua

Eating

Zairo   ITALIAN €
(☑049 66 38 03; zairo.net; Prato della Valle 51; pizzas €4-9.40, meals €25; ☺noon-2pm & 7pm-midnight Tue-Sun) The fresco above the kitchen door at this sweeping, chintzy restaurant-pizzeria dates back to 1673. But you're here for Zairo's cult hit *gnocchi verdi con gorgonzola* (spinach and potato gnocchi drizzled in a decadent gorgonzola sauce), or one of its decent, spot-hitting pizzas.

Osteria dei Fabbri   OSTERIA €€
(☑049 65 03 36; Via dei Fabbri 13; meals €30; ☺noon-2.30pm & 7-10.30pm Mon-Sat, noon-3pm Sun) Communal tables, wine-filled tumblers and a single-sheet menu packed with hearty dishes keep things real at dei Fabbri. Slurp on superlative *zuppe* (soups) such as sweet red-onion soup, or tuck into comforting meat dishes such as oven-roasted pork shank with Marsala, sultanas and polenta.

Belle Parti   ITALIAN €€€
(☑049 875 18 22; www.ristorantebelleparti.it; Via Belle Parti 11; meals €50; ☺12.30-2.30pm & 7.30-10.30pm Mon-Sat) Prime seasonal produce, impeccable wines and near-faultless service meld into one unforgettable whole at this stellar fine-dining restaurant. Seafood is the forte, including an arresting *gran piatto di crudità di mare* (raw seafood platter).

Drinking & Entertainment

Caffè Pedrocchi   CAFE
(☑049 878 12 31; www.caffepedrocchi.it; Via VIII Febbraio 15; ☺8.45am-midnight Apr-Oct, to 11pm Nov-Mar) Divided into three rooms – red, white and green – the neoclassical Pedrocchi has long been a seat of intrigue and revolution, as well as a favourite of Stendhal. Soak up its esteemed history over coffee or head in for a sprightly *spritz* and decent *aperitivo* snacks.

Decorated in styles ranging from ancient Egyptian to Imperial, the building's 1st floor is home to the **Museo del Risorgimento e dell'Età Contemporanea** (☑049 878 12 31; Galleria Pedrocchi 11; adult/child €4/2.50; ☺9.30am-12.30pm & 3.30-6pm Tue-Sun).

Enoteca Il Tira Bouchon   WINE BAR
(☑049 875 21 38; www.enotecapadova.it; Sotto il Salone 23/24; ☺10am-2.30pm & 5-9pm Mon-Sat) You can be sure of an excellent *prosecco*, Franciacorta or sauvignon at this traditional wine bar beneath Palazzo Ragione's arcades. There's a rotating selection of 12 wines by the glass. You'll find around 300 wines on the shelves, including some from emerging winemakers.

❶ Information

Hospital (☑049 821 11 11; Via Giustiniani 1) Main public hospital.

Police Station (☑049 83 31 11; Piazzetta Palatucci 5)

Tourist Office (☑049 201 00 80; www. turismopadova.it; Vicolo Pedrocchi; ☺9am-7pm Mon-Sat) Ask about the PadovaCard discount card here. There is a second **tourist office** (☑049 201 00 80; Piazza di Stazione; ☺9am-7pm Mon-Sat, 10am-4pm Sun) at the train station.

❶ Getting Around

TRAM
It is easy to get to all the sights by foot from the train and bus stations, but the city's single-branch tram running from the train station passes within 100m of all the main sights. Tickets (€1.30) are available at tobacconists and newsstands.

Turin & Genoa

Turin is an elegant city of baroque palaces, galleries and fabulous dining. Just a couple of hours south is Italy's Riviera and the port city of Genoa. Here dramatic coastal topography, beautifully preserved architecture and one of Italy's most memorable cuisines make for an impossibly romantic destination.

TURIN

POP 911,800 / ELEV 240M

There's a whiff of Paris in Turin's elegant tree-lined boulevards and echoes of Vienna in its stately art nouveau cafes, but make no mistake – this elegant, Alp-fringed city is utterly self-possessed. The innovative Torinese gave the world its first saleable hard chocolate, perpetuated one of its greatest mysteries (the Holy Shroud), popularised a best-selling car (the Fiat) and inspired the black-and-white stripes of one of the planet's most iconic football teams (Juventus).

Turin also gave the world Italy as we know it: Piedmont, with its wily Torinese president, the Count of Cavour, was the engine room of the Risorgimento (literally 'the Resurgence', referring to Italian unification). Turin also briefly served as Italy's first capital and donated its monarchy – the House of Savoy – to the newly unified Italian nation in 1861.

The 2006 Winter Olympics shook the city from a deep postindustrial malaise and sparked an urban revival, with a cultural knock-on effect that has seen an art, architecture and design scene blossom in the city.

◉ Sights

Museo Egizio　　　　　　　　　　MUSEUM
(Egyptian Museum;; www.museoegizio.it; Via Accademia delle Scienze 6; adult/reduced €13/9; ☺8.30am-7.30pm Tue-Sun, 9am-2pm Mon) Opened in 1824 and housed in the austere Palazzo

dell'Accademia delle Scienze, this Turin institution houses the most important collection of Egyptian treasure outside Cairo. Among its many highlights are a statue of Ramses II (one of the world's most important pieces of Egyptian art), the world's largest papyrus collection and over 500 funerary and domestic items from 1400 BC found in 1906 in the tomb of royal architect Kha and his wife Merit.

Mole Antonelliana　　　　　　　LANDMARK
(Via Montebello 20; panoramic lift adult/reduced €7/5, incl Museo €14/11; ☺lift 10am-8pm Tue-Fri & Sun, to 11pm Sat) The symbol of Turin, this 167m tower with its distinctive aluminium spire appears on the Italian two-cent coin. It was originally intended as a synagogue when construction began in 1862, but was never used as a place of worship, and nowadays houses the **Museo Nazionale del Cinema** (www.museocinema.it; ☺9am-8pm Tue-Fri & Sun, to 11pm Sat). For dazzling 360-degree views, take the **Panoramic Lift** up to the 85m-high outdoor viewing deck.

Museo Nazionale del Risorgimento Italiano　　　　　　MUSEUM
(www.museorisorgimentotorino.it; Via Accademia delle Scienze 5; adult/reduced €10/8; ☺10am-6pm Tue-Sun) After extensive renovations, this significant museum reopened in 2011 to coincide with the centenary of the Risorgimento

(reunification). An astounding 30-room trajectory illustrates the creation of the modern Italian state in the very building – the baroque Palazzo Carignano – where many of the key events happened. Not only was this the birthplace of Carlo Alberto and Vittorio Emanuele II, but it was also the seat of united Italy's first parliament from 1861 to 1864.

Duomo di San Giovanni
CATHEDRAL

(Piazza San Giovanni; ⊙8am-7pm Mon-Sat) Turin's cathedral was built between 1491 and 1498 on the site of three 14th-century basilicas and, before that, a Roman theatre. Plain interior aside, as home to the Shroud of Turin (alleged to be the burial cloth in which Jesus' body was wrapped) this is a highly trafficked church. A copy of the cloth is on permanent display to the left of the cathedral altar.

Museo della Sindone
MUSEUM

(www.sindone.org; Via San Domenico 28; adult/reduced €6/5; ⊙9am-noon & 3-7pm) Encased in the crypt of Santo Sudario church, this fascinating museum documents one of the most studied objects in human history: the Shroud of Turin. Despite the shroud's dubious authenticity, its story unfolds like a gripping suspense mystery, with countless plots, subplots and revelations.

Palazzo Reale
MUSEUM

See p21

Galleria Civica d'Arte Moderna e Contemporanea
ART GALLERY

(GAM; www.gamtorino.it; Via Magenta 31; adult/reduced €10/8; ⊙10am-6pm Tue-Sun) GAM was one of Italy's first modern art museums and has an astounding 45,000 works in its vaults dedicated to 19th- and 20th-century artists, including De Chirico, Otto Dix and Klee. It's a great place to expand your knowledge of Italy's postwar period: Paolini, Boetti, Anselmo, Penone and Pistoletto are all represented.

Parco Valentino
PARK

Opened in 1856 this 550,000-sq-m French-style park kisses the banks of the Po and and is filled with joggers, promenaders and lovers night and day. Walking southwest along the river brings you to Castello del Valentino (open for events only), a gorgeous mock chateau built in the 17th century.

Museo Nazionale dell'Automobile
MUSEUM

(☑011 67 76 66; www.museoauto.it; Corso Unità d'Italia 40; adult/reduced €8/6; ⊙10am-7pm Wed,

Mole Antonelliana
LADIRAS / GETTY IMAGES ©

Thu & Sun, to 9pm Fri & Sat, to 2pm Mon, 2-7pm Tue; Ⓜ Lingotto) As the historic birthplace of one of the world's leading car manufacturers – the 'T' in Fiat stands for Torino – Turin is the obvious place for a car museum. And this dashing modern museum, located roughly 5km south of the city centre, doesn't disappoint with its precious collection of over 200 automobiles – everything from an 1892 Peugeot to a 1980 Ferrari 308 (red, of course).

Basilica di Superga
BASILICA

(www.basilicadisuperga.com; Strada della Basilica di Superga 73) FREE Vittorio Amedeo II's 1706 promise, to build a basilica to honour the Virgin Mary if Turin was saved from besieging French and Spanish armies, resulted in this wedding cake edifice.

Architect Filippo Juvarra's Basilica di Superga became the final resting place of the Savoy family, whose lavish tombs make for interesting viewing, as does the dome. In 1949 the basilica gained less welcome renown when a plane carrying the entire Turin football team crashed into the church in thick fog, killing all on board. Their tomb rests at the rear of the church.

To get here take tram 15 from Piazza Vittorio Veneto to the Sassi–Superga stop on Corso Casale, then walk 20m to Stazione Sassi (Strada Comunale di Superga 4), from where an original 1934 tram (one way €4-6, return €6-9; ⊙hr vary) rattles the 3.1km up the hillside in 18 minutes, every day except Tuesday.

Turin

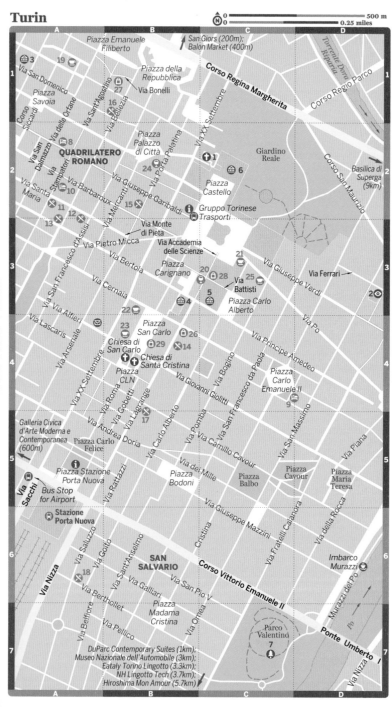

0 500 m
0 0.25 miles

Piazza Emanuele Filiberto

San Giors (200m);
Balon Market (400m)

Corso Regina Margherita

Torrente Dora Riparia

Corso Regio Parco

Piazza della Repubblica

Via Bonelli

Piazza Savoia

Via San Domenico

Corso Siccardi

Via Sant'Agostino

Via delle Orfane

Via Venezia

Piazza Palazzo di Città

Via XX Settembre

Giardino Reale

Corso San Maurizio

Basilica di Superga (9km)

QUADRILATERO ROMANO

Via San Dalmazzo

Via Stampatori

Via Barbaroux

Via Santa Maria

Via Giuseppe Garibaldi

Via Porta Palatina

Piazza Castello

Gruppo Torinese Trasporti

Via Mercanti

Via Monte di Pietà

Via Pietro Micca

Via Accademia delle Scienze

Via Giuseppe Verdi

Via Ferrari

Via Bertola

Piazza Carignano

Via Cernaia

Piazza Carlo Alberto

Piazza Carlo Emanuele II

Via San Francesco d'Assisi

Via Alfieri

Via Lascaris

Via Arsenale

Piazza San Carlo

Chiesa di San Carlo

Chiesa di Santa Cristina

Piazza CLN

Via Battisti

Via Po

Via Principe Amedeo

Piazza Carlo Emanuele II

Via XX Settembre

Via Roma

Via Gobetti

Via Lagrange

Via Giovanni Giolitti

Via Bogino

Via San Francesco da Paola

Via San Massimo

Galleria Civica d'Arte Moderna e Contemporanea (600m)

Piazza Carlo Felice

Via Andrea Doria

Via Carlo Alberto

Via dei Mille

Via Pomba

Via Camillo Cavour

Piazza Cavour

Via Piana

Piazza Stazione Porta Nuova

Bus Stop for Airport

Via Sacchi

Stazione Porta Nuova

Via Rattazzi

Piazza Bodoni

Piazza Balbo

Via Giuseppe Mazzini

Piazza Maria Teresa

Via della Rocca

Via Nizza

Via Saluzzo

Via Goito

Via Sant'Anselmo

SAN SALVARIO

Via Galliari

Via San Pio V

Corso Vittorio Emanuele II

Via Fratelli Calandra

Imbarco Murazzi

Via Belfiore

Via Berthollet

Via Pellico

Piazza Madama Cristina

Via Omea

Cristina

Parco Valentino

Po

Murazzi del Po

Ponte Umberto I

Via Nizza

DuParc Contemporary Suites (1km);
Museo Nazionale dell'Automobile (3km);
Eataly Torino Lingotto (3.3km);
NH Lingotto Tech (3.7km);
Hiroshima Mon Amour (5.7km)

Turin

👉 Tours

Turismo Bus Torino   BUS
(www.gtt.to.it; 1-day tickets adult/child €20/10, Line C €10/5, 2-day tickets €25/12, all 3 lines €30/15; ⊙10am-6pm) This bus service with audioguides in English has a central stop on Piazza Castello at the corner of Via Po. Line A serves over a dozen points around central Turin, Line B takes in Lingotto and other southern attractions and Line C covers Reggia di Venaria Reale, Rivoli and the Juventus stadium.

Navigazione sul Po   BOAT
(return €4-9) Grupo Torinese Transporti operates boat trips on the Po. Boats to the Borgo Medievale in Parco Valentino and on to Museo Nazionale dell'Automobile depart from **Imbarco Murazzi** (Murazzi del Po 65) four to

nine times daily in summer and on weekends in winter.

Somewhere   WALKING TOUR
(www.somewhere.it) Turin's alleged 'black and white magic' is illuminated on a quirky walking tour, Torino Magica (€22), and its underbelly is examined during Underground Turin (€28). You can opt for more traditional food or royal palace tours if the dark arts aren't your cup of chocolate. Confirm departure points when booking.

⭐ Festivals & Events

The tourist office has details of these and other events.

Salone Internazionale del Libro di Torino   BOOK FAIR
(en.salonelibro.it) Held every May, Turin's book fair is one of the most important in Europe.

Salone Internazionale del Gusto   FOOD
(www.salonedelgusto.it) Every October in even-numbered years, food-lovers roll into town for this Slow Food talk-and-taste fest, with traditional producers from around the world showcasing their wares at Lingotto Fiere. Day passes cost around €20.

Cioccolatò   FOOD
(www.cioccola-to.it) Turin celebrates chocolate and its status as a world chocolate capital in late November.

🛏 Sleeping

Via Stampatori   B&B €
(☑339 2581330; www.viastampatori.com; Via Stampatori 4; s/d €70/110; 🛜) This utterly lovely B&B occupies the top floor of a frescoed Renaissance building. Six bright, stylish and uniquely furnished rooms overlook either a sunny terrace or a leafy inner courtyard. The owner's personal collection of 20th-century design is used throughout the rooms and several serene common areas. It's central but blissfully quiet.

San Giors   BOUTIQUE HOTEL €
(☑011 521 63 57; www.hotelsangiors.it; Via Borgo Dora 3; s/d €75/99; 🛜) If you're not perturbed by a still-gentrifying neighbourhood, this small, welcoming family-run place offers rooms that are basic but elegantly furnished with beautiful vintage design pieces and a witty, bohemian eye. Its restaurant comes highly recommended, and come Saturday, you're in the thick of the Balon, one of Italy's best flea markets. Breakfast is €8 extra.

DuParc
Contemporary Suites   DESIGN HOTEL €€

(☑ 011 650 83 83; www.duparcsuites.com; Corso Massimo D'Azeglio 21; d/ste €135/145; P ❋ 🕿) A business-friendly location doesn't mean this isn't a great choice for all travellers. The building's stark modern lines are softened with a fantastic contemporary art collection, bold colour and tactile furnishings. Best of all, even the cheapest rooms here are sumptuously large, with king beds, ample cupboard space, huge baths and floor-to-ceiling windows.

Le Due Matote   B&B €€

(Via Garibaldi 31; s/d €100/130; ❋ 🕿) Perched above Turin's favourite *passeggiata* parade, this elegant B&B is a bastion of calm, with three classically decorated rooms with features that are rare at this price: Nespresso machines in all rooms, marble-topped baths in the two larger ones and a lushly planted terrace with the largest of them all.

NH Piazza Carlina   DESIGN HOTEL €€€

(☑ 848 390230; www.nh-hotels.com; Piazza Carlo Emanuele II; s/d €180/220) On one of Turin's most beautiful squares, this sprawling property occupies a 17th-century building, once the Albergo di Virtù, a Savoy charitable institution; it also once housed the political theorist Antonio Gramsci. The decor is cutting edge, highly atmospheric and deeply luxurious. Guests have access to rooftop terraces, and breakfast is served in a stately courtyard.

NH Lingotto Tech   BUSINESS HOTEL €€€

(☑ 011 664 20 00; www.nh-hotels.com; Via Nizza 262; d €200; P ❋ 🕿) This old Fiat factory hotel comes with a unique perk: the 1km running track on the roof is Fiat's former testing track and featured in the film *The Italian Job*. Its 20th-century industrial bones also mean rooms are huge and bright; the fit-out is slick, high-naughties industrial, too. As a corporate favourite, its facilities are comprehensive and include a 24-hour gym.

Eating

Turin is blessed with a hinterland fabulously rich in produce and tradition along with an increasing number of young and innovative restaurateurs and chefs. Specialities include *risotto alla piemontese* (risotto with butter and cheese), *vitello tonnato* (veal with tuna sauce) and panna cotta as well as *tajarin* (a thin tagliatelle). Sushi and sushi hybrids are also Torinese favourites.

Eataly Incontra   PIEDMONT, SUPERMARKET €

(☑ 011 037 32 21; www.eataly.net; Via Lagrange 3; €18-25; ☺ noon-10.30pm, cafe from 8am, shop from 10am) Perfect for a casual lunch or dinner, this mini-Eataly has shaded tables on the lovely pedestrian stretch of Lagrange. Food is fresh, simple and quick – think octopus and potato salad, *cruda* (raw minced steak), or linguine with pistachio pesto and stracciatella cheese – and the drinks list includes sulphur-free wines and artisan beers.

È Cucina   MODERN ITALIAN €

(www.cesaremarretti.com; Via Bertola 27a; meals €25; ☺ noon-2pm & 7-10pm) Northern Italians are fond of a 'concept' and Bolognese chef Cesare Marretti's concept here is *sorpesa* (surprise). Beyond the choice of meat, fish or vegetables and the number of courses you want, it's up to the kitchen. What *is* certain is the innovative cooking and excellent produce that will arrive. Local's tip: don't be tempted to over order.

SLOW FOOD

Slow Food was the 1980s brainchild of a group of disenchanted Italian journalists from the Piemontese town of Bra. United by their taste buds, they ignited a global crusade against the fast-food juggernaut threatening to engulf Italy's centuries-old gastronomic heritage. Their mantra was pleasure over speed and taste over convenience in a manifesto that promoted sustainability, local produce and the protection of long-standing epicurean traditions. Paradoxically, Slow Food grew quickly after its 1987 inauguration and by the early 2000s it was sponsoring more restaurants in Piedmont than McDonald's. In 2004 its founder, Carlo Petrini, set up a University of Gastronomic Sciences in Pollenzo as a way of passing the baton on to future generations. The mindset worked. Today Slow Food counts 100,000 members in 150 countries and has attracted big-name affiliates, such as Turin-founded supermarket company Eataly and popular ice-cream manufacturer Grom, as well as dozens of characterful and refreshingly slow restaurants – all of them simultaneously tradition-bound and forward looking.

Perino Vesco
BAKERY €

(☑ 011 068 60 56; www.perinovesco.it; Via Cavour 10; snacks from €5; ⊗ 7.30am-7.30pm Mon-Sat) 🏴 Cult Slow Food baker Andrea Perino turns out the city's best *grissini* (bread sticks) along with dense, fragrant *torta langarola* (hazelnut cake), naturallly yeasted *panettone* and focaccia that draws sighs from homesick Ligurians. Join the queues for takeaway pizza and focaccia slices or head out the back and try to nab a seat for sandwiches, pizza slices, savoury tarts and coffee.

Gofri Piemontéisa
SNACKS €

(www.gofriemiassepiemontesi.it; Via San Tommaso 4a; €4.40-5; ⊗ 11.30am-7.30pm Mon-Sat) 🏴 *Gofri* (thin waffles snap cooked in hot irons) are a traditional dish from the mountainous regions of northern Piedmont and have been reinvented here by a local chef as tasty fast food. Try the house *gofre* with ham, *toma* (alpine cheese) and artichokes or one of the equally delicious *miasse*, a corn-based variant, also adapted from ancient recipes.

Banco vini e alimenti
PIEDMONT €€

(☑ 011 764 02 39; www.bancoviniealimenti.it; Via dei Mercanti 13f; €25-28) A new breed hybrid restaurant-bar-deli, this smartly designed but low-key place does clever small-dish dining for lunch and dinner. While it might vibe casual wine bar, with young staff in T-shirts and boyfriend jeans, don't underestimate the food: this is serious Piedmontese cooking. It's open all day, so you can grab a single-origin pour-over here in the morning, or a herbal house *spritz* late afternoon.

Consorzio
PIEDMONT €€

(☑ 011 276 76 61; ristoranteconsorzio.com; Via Monte Pietà 23; mains €30-40, set menus €32; ⊗ 12.30-2.30pm Mon-Fri, 7.30-11pm Mon-Sat) It can be almost impossible to secure a table at this Quadrilatero Romano institution. Do book ahead, don't expect flash decor and pay the not-always-accomodating staff no mind. Everyone is here for the pristine, well sourced, spot-on Piedmontese cooking that's so traditional it's innovative. The wine list, too, is thoughtful and occasionally provocative, and much of it is sourced from a family vineyard.

Scannabue
PIEDMONT €€

(☑ 011 669 66 93; www.scannabue.it; Largo Saluzzo 25h; meals €35; ⊗ 12.30-2.30pm & 7.30-10.30pm) Scannabue, housed in a former corner garage, is a retro-fitted bistro that has a touch of Paris in its cast-iron doors and tiled floors. There's a casual feel, but the cooking is some of Turin's most lauded.

Staples like *baccalà* (cod) are freshly matched with Jerusalem artichoke puree and crisped leeks, a starter reworks the French *tarte Tatin* into thoroughly modern onion pie, and there's a club sandwich on offer if you miss service.

L'Acino
PIEDMONT €€

(☑ 011 521 70 77; Via San Domenico 2a; meals €35-40; ⊗ 7.30-11.30pm Mon-Sat) Half a dozen tables and a legion of enamoured followers mean this inviting restaurant is hard to get into. Book ahead or arrive at the stroke of 7.30pm for snails, tripe and *ragù* (meat stew) cooked in Roero wine, or classic Piedmontese pasta staples such as *plin* (ravioli). The *bonet* (chocolate pudding) is considered one of the city's best.

🍷 Drinking & Nightlife

Aperitivi and more substantial *apericenas* are a Turin institution – this is the home of vermouth, after all. If you're on a tight budget, you can fill up on a generous buffet of bar snacks for the cost of a drink. Nightlife concentrates in the riverside area around Piazza Vittoria Veneto, the Quadrilatero Romano district and increasingly the southern neighbourhoods of San Salvarino and Vanchiglia.

Al Bicerin
CAFE, CHOCOLATE

(www.bicerin.it; Piazza della Consolata 5; ⊗ 8.30am-7.30pm Thu-Tue, closed Aug) Founded in 1763, with an exquisitely simple wood-panelled interior dating to the early 1800s, this one-room cafe takes its name from its signature drink, a potent combination of chocolate, coffee and cream. It fuelled the likes of Dumas, Puccini, Nietzsche and Calvino, along with Savoy royalty and Turin's workers – the price didn't rise for a century to ensure no one missed out.

Caffè Mulassano
CAFE

(Piazza Castello 15; ⊗ 7.30am-10.30pm) Elbow your way to the bar or hope for a seat at one of the five wee tables at this art-nouveau gem, where regulars sink espresso *in piedi* (standing) while discussing Juventus' current form with the bow-tied baristas.

Caffè San Carlo
CAFE

See p20

Balon flea market

FRANCISCO GONÇALVES / GETTY IMAGES ©

Caffè Torino   CAFE

(Piazza San Carlo 204; ⊙7.30am-1am) This chandelier-lit showpiece opened in 1903. A brass plaque of the city's emblem, a bull (*torino* means 'little bull'), is embedded in the pavement out front; rub your shoe across it for good luck.

Fiorio   CAFE

(Via Po 8; ⊙8.30am-1am Tue-Sun) Garner literary inspiration in Mark Twain's old window seat as you contemplate the gilded interior of a cafe where 19th-century students plotted revolutions and the Count of Cavour played whist. The bittersweet hot chocolate remains inspirational.

Bar Cavour   COCKTAIL BAR

(Del Cambio; ☑011 54 66 90; delcambio.it; Piazza Carignano 2; 7pm-1.30am Tue-Sat) Named for its most famous barfly, the ubiquitous Count of Cavour, this beautiful room combines a magical, mirrored historical setting with a great collection of contemporary art and design savvy. Upstairs from Del Cambio, a Michelin-starred restaurant, the *aperitivo* here doesn't come cheap but is an elegant respite from pizza slices. There's a bar menu until midnight too (it can be hard to tear yourself away from such luxury).

Caffè-Vini Emilio Ranzini   WINE BAR

(☑011 765 04 77; Via Porta Palatina 9g; ⊙9.30am-8.30pm Mon-Fri, 10.30am-5pm Sat) Location scouts looking for a neighbourhood bar from Turin's mid-century glory days would jump on this little place. A crew of local shopkeepers, creatives and students frequently prop up its dark wooden bar and loll about the summer courtyard with wines by the glass, €1 boiled eggs and small plates.

Hiroshima Mon Amour   CLUB

(www.hiroshimamonamour.org; Via Bossoli 83; admission free–€15; ⊙hr vary) This legendary dance club features everything from folk and punk to tango and techno. Check the website for opening hours.

☆ Entertainment

Teatro Regio Torino   THEATRE

(☑011 881 52 41; www.teatroregio.torino.it; Piazza Castello 215; ⊙ticket office 10.30am-6pm Tue-Fri, to 4pm Sat & 1hr before performances) Sold-out performances can sometimes be watched free on live TV in the adjoining Teatro Piccolo Regio, where Puccini premiered *La Bohème* in 1896. Sadly, much of Carlo Molino's visionary mid-century fit-out did not survive subsequent renovations, but it's still worth a peek. Ticket prices start at €55.

Spazio 211   LIVE MUSIC

(☑011 1970 5919; www.spazio211.com; Via Cigna 21) This long-established live music venue, a 10-minute taxi ride north of the city centre, is the city's main venue for international indie acts, interesting theme nights, and big names like Guida. Book tickets on the website.

🛍 Shopping

Eataly Torino Lingotto CAFE, SUPERMARKET
(www.eataly.net; Via Nizza 230; ⊙10am-10.30pm)
⬤ The global Slow Food phenomena began
here in Lingotto. Set in a vast converted factory, the Eataly mothership houses a staggering array of sustainable food and drink, along
with kitchenware and cookbooks. Specialist
counters that correspond to their produce
area – bread and pizza, cheese, pasta, seafood, Piedmontese beef – serve lunch from
12.30pm to 2.30pm. Food lovers heaven!

Guido Gobino CHOCOLATE
(www.guidogobino.it; Via Lagrange 1; ⊙10am-8pm
Tue-Sun, 3-8pm Mon) ⬤ Relative newcomer
Guido Gobino's extreme attention to detail,
flair and innovation have made him Turin's
favourite chocolatier. Have a box of his tiny
tile-like ganache chocolates made to order:
highly evocative flavours include vermouth,
Barolo and lemon and clove, or grab a bag
of his classic *gianduiotto* (triangular chocolates made from *gianduja* – Turin's hazelnut paste).

Laboratorio Zanzara CRAFTS
(⬤011 026 88 53; www.laboratoriozanzara.it; Via
Bonelli 3a; ⊙10am-12.30pm & 2-4pm Mon-Fri,
10am-12.30pm & 3.30-7pm Sat) A delightfully
eccentric collection of handmade objects,
light fittings, posters and calendars fill this
shop, which is run as a nonprofit cooperative, employing people with intellectual disabilities. It's a noble enterprise, yes, but its
wares are the model of Torinese cool, with
the co-op's director, Gianluca Cannizzo, also
one of the city's most celebrated creatives.

Balon MARKET
(www.balon.it; Via Borgo Dora; ⊙7am-7pm Sat)
This sprawling flea market has brought
street merchants to the north of Porta Palazzo for over 150 years. It's both fascinating
and overwhelming, but can turn up some
splendid vintage finds for the persistent and
sharp of eye. The pace settles down come
midafternoon and there are plenty of art-
fully dishevelled cafes and bars at which to
grab a coffee or *spritz*.

Libreria Luxemburg BOOKS
(Via Battisti 7; ⊙9am-7.30pm Mon-Sat, 10am-1pm &
3-7pm Sun) This dark, rambling Anglophone
bookshop is stocked with literary fiction, light
reading, international magazines and a full
stash of travel guides, including Lonely Planet
guidebooks. They also carry UK newspapers.

San Carlo dal 1973 FASHION
(San Carlo 1; ⬤011 511 41 11; www.sancarlodal1973.
com; Piazza San Carlo 201; ⊙3-7pm Mon,
10.30am-7pm Tue-Sat) This Torinese fashion
institution – the city's first 'concept store' –
stocks a tightly curated selection of Italian
and European high fashion, along with a
selection of perfumes and candles. It's Turin
at its most elegant and worth a wander for
the architecture and people-watching alone.

ℹ Information

A bank, ATM and exchange booth can all be
found within Stazione Porta Nuova.

Farmacia Boniscontro (⬤011 53 82 71; Corso
Vittorio Emanuele II 66; ⊙9am-12.30pm &
3.30-9.30pm)

Ospedale Mauriziano Umberto I (Hospital;
⬤011 5 08 01; Largo Turati 62)

Piazza Carlo Felice Tourist Office (⬤011 53
51 81; Piazza Carlo Felice; ⊙9am-7pm) On the
piazza in front of Stazione Porta Nuova.

Piazza Castello Tourist Office (⬤011 53 51
81; www.turismotorino.org; Piazza Castello;
⊙9am-7pm) Central and multilingual.

Police Station (⬤011 5 58 81; Corso Vinzaglio 10)

ℹ Getting There & Around

AIR

Turin Airport (Caselle; www.turin-airport.com;
Strada Aeroporto 12) Turin's airport, 16km
northwest of the city centre in Caselle, has
connections to national and European destinations. Budget airline Ryanair operates flights to
London Stansted, Barcelona, Berlin and Ibiza.

TO/FROM THE AIRPORT

Sadem (www.sadem.it) runs buses to the airport
from Stazione Porta Nuova (one way/return
€7.50/12, 40 minutes), also stopping at Stazione
Porta Susa (30 minutes). Buses depart every 30

ℹ **PIEDMONT DISCOUNT
CARD**

Serious sightseers will save a bundle
with a Torino+Piemonte Card (one/
two/three/five days €23/35/42/51). It
covers admission to 190 of the region's
monuments and museums, and offers
reductions on various forms of public
transport, including Turin's Sassi–
Superga tram, GTT boats on the Po
river and the Turismo Bus Torino. It also
offers discounts on some guided tours
and theatres. You can buy the card at
Turin's tourist office.

minutes between 5.15am and 10.30pm and run from 6.10am to midnight from the airport.

A taxi between the airport and the city centre will cost around €40 to €50.

CAR & MOTORCYCLE

Major car-rental agencies have offices at Stazione Porta Nuova and the airport.

PUBLIC TRANSPORT

Genoa has a network of buses, trams, a cable car and a small metro system, all run by the **Gruppo Torinese Trasporti** (GTT; Map p164; www.gtt.to.it/en; Piazza Castello; ⊙10am-6pm), which has an **information office** (⊙7am-9pm) at Stazione Porta Nuova. Buses and trams run from 6am to midnight and tickets cost €1 (€13.50 for a 15-ticket carnet and €3.50 for a one-day pass).

Turin's single-line metro runs from Fermi to Lingotto. It first opened for the Winter Olympics in February 2006 and reached Lingotto in 2011. The line will extend south to Piazza Bengazi, two stations south of Lingotto (ETA 2017). Tickets cost €1.50 and allow 90-minute connections with bus and tram networks.

TAXI

Radio Taxi (☑011 57 30; www.radiotaxi.it) Flagfall €3.50, night fee €2.50.

GENOA

POP 583,500

Genoa's name is thought to come from the Latin *ianua*, 'door'. Founded in the 4th century BC, it was an important Roman port and was later occupied by Franks, Saracens and the Milanese, but as the Mediterranean's mercantile importance declined, so did Genoa.

Christopher Columbus is Genoa's most famous son, and in 1992 the 500th anniversary of his seminal voyage to America transformed Genoa's ancient harbour from a decaying backwater into a showpiece for the city. Renzo Piano orchestrated the overhaul, adding a number of striking permanent attractions; just over a decade later, in 2004, Genoa was named a European City of Culture.

☉ Sights

Aside from the Ligurian cuisine, Genoa's tour de force is its Palazzi dei Rolli. Forty-two of these lodging palaces – built between 1576 and 1664 to host visiting European gentry – were placed on the Unesco World Heritage list in 2006. They are mostly on or around Via Garibaldi and Via Balbi.

Palazzo Reale PALACE, MUSEUM
See p22

Musei di Strada Nuova MUSEUM
(www.museidigenova.it; Via Garibaldi; adult/reduced €9/7; ⊙9am-7pm Tue, Wed & Fri, to 9pm Thu, 9.30am-7pm Sat & Sun) Skirting the northern edge of what was once the city limits, pedestrianised Via Garibaldi (formerly called the Strada Nuova) was planned by Galeazzo Alessi in the 16th century. It quickly became the city's most sought-after quarter, lined with the palaces of Genoa's wealthiest citizens. Three of these palazzi – Rosso, Bianco and Doria-Tursi – today comprise the Musei di Strada Nuova. Between them, they hold the city's finest collection of old masters.

Cattedrale di San Lorenzo CATHEDRAL
(Piazza San Lorenzo; ⊙8am-noon & 3-7pm) Genoa's zebra-striped Gothic-Romanesque cathedral owes its continued existence to the poor quality of a British WWII bomb that failed to ignite here in 1941; it still sits to the side of the nave like an innocuous museum piece.

Palazzo Ducale MUSEUM
See p49

**Piazza de Ferrari &
Palazzo della Borsa** PIAZZA
See p48

Old City NEIGHBOURHOOD
The heart of medieval Genoa – bounded by ancient city gates Porta dei Vacca and Porta Soprana, and the streets of Via Cairoli, Via Garibaldi and Via XXV Aprile – is famed for its *caruggi* (narrow lanes). Looking up at the washing pegged on lines everywhere, it becomes obvious that these dark, cavelike lanes and blind alleys are still largely residential, although the number of fashionable bars, shops and cafes continues to grow.

Parts of the *caruggi* can feel unnerving, especially after dark. Although it's not particularly dangerous, take care in the zone west of Via San Luca and south to Piazza Banchi, where most street prostitution and accompanying vice concentrates. East of the piazza is Via Orefici, where you'll find market stalls.

Casa della Famiglia Colombo MUSEUM
(Piazza Dante; admission €6; ⊙9am-noon & 2-6pm Sat & Sun) Not the only house claiming to be the birthplace of the navigator Christopher Columbus (Calvi in Corsica is another contender), this one probably has the most merit, as various documents inside testify. Curiously, it stands just outside the old city

walls in the shadow of the Porta Soprana gate (built in 1155).

Palazzo Spinola &
Galleria Nazionale　　ART GALLERY
See p22

Porto Antico　　NEIGHBOURHOOD
See p48

Galata Museo del Mare　　MUSEUM
(www.galatamuseodelmare.it; Calata de Mari 1; admission €11; ⊙10am-7.30pm, closed Mon Nov-Feb) Genoa was rivalled only by Barcelona and Venice as a medieval and Renaissance maritime power; not surprisingly, its 'museum of the sea' is one of its most relevant and interesting. High-tech exhibits trace the history of seafaring, from its reign as Europe's greatest dockyard to the ages of sail and steam.

☞ Tours

Information and tickets for boat trips around the port and to destinations further afield are available from the **ticket booths** (Ponte Spinola; ⊙9.30am-6.30pm Sep-Jun, 9am-8pm Jul & Aug) at Porto Antico. The tourist office has information on walking tours and guided walks of the historic centre, including one exploring its traditional shops.

Whale Watch Liguria　　WHALE WATCHING
(www.whalewatchliguria.it; tickets €33; ⊙1.30pm Sat Apr-Oct) These five-hour spring and summer tours are run in consultation with the WWF and include fascinating background on the world's largest mammals provided by an on-board biologist.

Genova City Sightseeing　　BUS TOUR
(www.genova.city-sightseeing.it; 2-day tickets €15) Hop-on, hop-off open-topped bus tours, with headphone commentary in five languages. Tickets are sold on the bus and stops are located in Piazza de Ferrari and Via XX Settembre. Runs March through November.

✹ Festivals & Events

Slow Fish　　FOOD
(slowfish.slowfood.it) 🌿 Every odd-numbered year in early May, this festival celebrates seafood with a fish market and tastings. Affiliated with the Slow Food Movement, it runs free workshops focusing on water pollution, good fishing practices and aquaculture.

Premio Paganini　　MUSIC
(www.premiopaganini.it; ⊙Sep) This international violin competition is held in homage

to Genoese violinist Niccolò Paganini (1782–1849). Performances are held in the Teatro Carlo Felice (p49).

🛏 Sleeping

Palazzo Cambiaso　　APARTMENT €
(My Place; ☑010 856 61 88; www.palazzocambiaso.it; Via al Ponte Calvi 6; d €110, apt €140-170) A real attention to design is evident in these rooms and apartments, set on the upper floor of a stately *palazzo*. The larger ones (sleeping up to six) come with full marble kitchens, long dining tables and laundries, but even the cheapest double is spacious, soothing and has the signature Frette linen.

Hotel Cristoforo Colombo　　HOTEL €
(☑010 251 36 43; www.hotelcolombo.it; Via di Porta Soprana 27; s/d €80/100; 🖧) A totally charming family-run hotel ideally situated near Cattedrale di San Lorenzo, Cristoforo Colombo has 18 colour-accented rooms with eclectic furnishings. Breakfast is served on an inviting 6th-floor rooftop terrace.

Le Nuvole　　BOUTIQUE HOTEL €€
(☑010 251 00 18; www.hotellenuvole.it; Piazza delle Vigne 6; d €130; ✳@🖧) This bright newcomer full of smart modern furniture and slick bathrooms makes the most of the original architecture of an ancient *palazzo*, with lofty ceilings, lovingly restored plaster mouldings and beautiful tilework. Owners are hands-on and helpful.

Quarto Piano　　B&B €€
(☑348 7426779; www.quarto-piano.it; Piazza Pellicceria 2/4; d/ste €130/165; ✳🖧) Four elegant, modern rooms share the 4th floor, complete with a terrace for breakfast or hot-tub dip.

Genoa

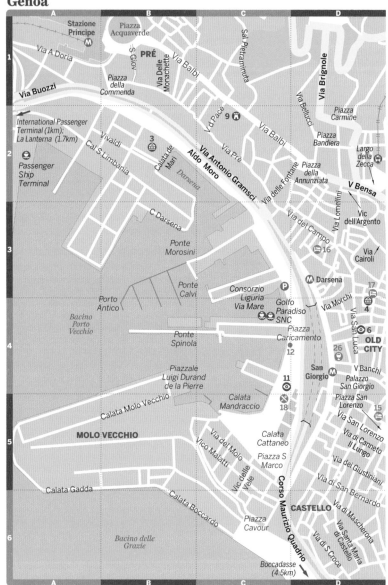

Locanda di Palazzo Cicala BOUTIQUE HOTEL €€
(☎ 010 251 88 24; www.palazzocicala.it; Piazza
San Lorenzo 16; d/ste €125/170; ❄@🖼) In
stark contrast to its grand 18th-century
stucco exterior, the six minimalist rooms
include pieces by Jasper Morrison and
Philippe Starck. Great stuff, but don't expect any TLC and make sure you get a firm
confirmation of where exactly you'll sleep,
as guests are often palmed out to adequate
but less appealing apartments in the surrounding streets.

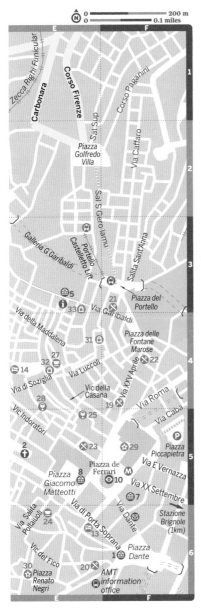

Genoa

◎ Sights

1	Casa della Famiglia Colombo	F6
2	Cattedrale di San Lorenzo	E5
3	Galata Museo del Mare	B2
4	Galleria Nazionale	D4
5	Musei di Strada Nuova	E3
6	Old City	D4
7	Palazzo della Borsa	F5
8	Palazzo Ducale	E5
9	Palazzo Reale	C2
	Palazzo Spinola	(see 4)
10	Piazza de Ferrari	F5
11	Porto Antico	C4

⊙ Activities, Courses & Tours

12	Whale Watch Liguria	C4

⊜ Sleeping

13	Hotel Cristoforo Colombo	E6
14	Le Nuvole	E4
15	Locanda di Palazzo Cicala	D5
16	Palazzo Cambiaso	D3
17	Quarto Piano	D3

⊗ Eating

18	Il Marin	C5
19	Le Dolcezze Salate Di Angelo	F4
20	Officina 34	E6
21	Pasticceria Profumo	F3
22	Trattoria Da Maria	F4
23	Trattoria Rosmarino	E5

⊖ Drinking & Nightlife

24	Café degli Specchi	E6
25	Cambi Cafe	E5
26	Enoteca Pesce	D4
27	Fratelli Klainguti	E4
28	Les Rouges	E4

⊛ Entertainment

29	Teatro Carlo Felice	F5
30	Teatro della Tosse	E6

⊜ Shopping

31	Butteghetta Magica di Tinello Daniela	E4
32	Pietro Romanengo fu Stefano	E4
33	Via Garibaldi 12	E3

✗ Eating

It would be criminal to come to Genoa and not try *pesto genovese*. The city's famous basil pesto really does taste, and look, better here than anywhere else, a result of the basil that's used (young plants are plucked daily from hothouses on city hillsides), as well as techniques honed through generations.

Trattoria Da Maria　　　　TRATTORIA €
(☑ 010 58 10 80; Vico Testadoro 14r; meals €15; ☺ 11.45am-3pm Mon-Sat, 7-9.30pm Thu & Fri) Brace yourself for lunchtime mayhem. This is a totally authentic, if well touristed, workers' trattoria and there's much squeezing into tiny tables, shouted orders and a fast and furious

101

ROSTISLAV GLINSKY / SHUTTERSTOCK ©

Teatro Carlo Felice

succession of plates plonked on tables. A daily hand-scrawled menu is a roll call of elemental favourites that keep patrons full and happy, along with the jugs of ridiculously cheap wine.

Le Dolcezze Salate Di Angelo
BAKERY €

(Via XXV Aprile 22; focaccias from €1.50; ⊘8am-3.30pm Tue-Sun) Every Genovese has a favourite focaccia spot, but this one gets recommended more than most. Pungent with Ligurian olive oil and spiked with flecks of sea salt, the basic model is moreish to a fault.

Pasticceria Profumo
PASTRIES €

(www.villa1827.it; Via del Portello 2; ⊘9am-1pm & 3.30-7.30pm Tue-Sat) A traditional *pasticceria* and chocolate shop that follows the seasons – chocolate, chestnuts and cream dominate in winter, fresh stone fruit and berries in summer – this is also one of Genoa's most pretty, with bright, stylish packaging that makes for fantastic take-home gifts.

Trattoria Rosmarino
TRATTORIA €€

(☑010 251 04 75; www.trattoriarosmarino.it; Salita del Fondaco 30; meals €30; ⊘noon-3pm & 7-11pm Mon-Sat) Rosmarino cooks up the standard local specialities, yes, but the straightforwardly priced menu has an elegance and vibrancy that set it apart. With two nightly sittings, there's always a nice buzz (though there's also enough nooks and crannies that a romantic night for two isn't out of the question). Call ahead for an evening table.

Officina 34
MODERN ITALIAN €€

(☑010 302 71 84; www.officina34.it; Via di Ravecca 34; meals €30) Genoa is a long way from Berlin or Brooklyn, but that urban aesthetic is in full force at Officina 34. Subway tile jokes aside, it's a beautifully fitted-out space in a pretty location, and has a simple, gently innovative menu that shows the kitchen cares about quality ingredients. A young, good-looking crowd comes for raw plates and *aperitivo* and often ends up staying late.

Il Marin
SEAFOOD €€€

(Eataly Genova; ☑010 869 87 22; www.eataly.net; Porto Antico; meals €50; ⊘noon-3pm & 7-10.30pm) Eating by the water often means a compromise in quality, but Eataly's 3rd-floor fine-dining space delivers both panoramic port views and Genoa's most innovative seafood menu. Rustic wooden tables, Renzo Piano–blessed furniture and an open kitchen make for an easy, relaxed glamour, while dishes use unusual Mediterranean-sourced produce and look gorgeous on the plate.

This is the destination restaurant the city has long needed. Book ahead.

🍷 Drinking & Nightlife

The revamped Porto Antico has an early night-time scene, but never underestimate the lure of the *caruggi* later on.

Les Rouges
COCKTAIL BAR

(☑010 246 49 56; www.lesrouges.it; Piazza Campetto 8a, 1st floor; ⊙5.30-11pm Tue-Thu & Sun, to 12.30am Fri & Sat) One of Genoa's surfeit of crumbling *palazzi* is being put to excellent use in this atmospheric cocktail bar. Three bearded, vest-wearing, red-headed brothers – the 'rouges' of the name – man the floor and shake up the city's only new-wave cocktails, using top-shelf ingredients and herbal or floral flavours like camomile and Kaffir lime.

Cambi Cafe
BAR

See p49

Enoteca Pesce
WINE BAR

(Via Sottoripa; ⊙8.30am-7.30pm Mon-Sat) Tiny wine bars dot Genoa's old city, although this one, under the arches by the port, is particularly characteristic, full of colourful locals and serious about its product. Glasses hover around the €2 mark, so it's a good place to get to know Liguria's unusual grapes.

Fratelli Klainguti
CAFE

(Via di Soziglia; ⊙8am-8pm) Predating cappuccinos, Klainguti opened in 1828 and its mitteleuropean charms, and presumably its strudel and pastries, had Verdi and Garibaldi coming back for more. Waiters in bow ties toil under a chandelier and the decor is a fabulous, if tatty, mid-century historical pastiche.

Café degli Specchi
CAFE

(Via Salita Pollaiuoli 43r; ⊙7am-9pm Mon-Sat) A bit of Turin disconnected and relocated 150km to the south, this tiled art-deco showpiece was (and is) a favourite hang-out of Genoa's intellectuals. You can sink your espresso at street level or disappear upstairs amid the velvet seats and mirrors for coffee, cake and an *aperitivo* buffet.

☆ Entertainment

At the western end of the Porto Antico, the Magazzini del Cotone (one-time cotton warehouses) have been converted into an entertainment area with a multiplex cinema, games arcade and shops.

Teatro Carlo Felice
THEATRE

See p49

Teatro della Tosse
THEATRE

(www.teatrodellatosse.it; Piazza Renato Negri 4) Casanova trod the boards of the city's oldest theatre, which dates from 1702.

🛍 Shopping

Heading southwest, elegant Via Roma, adjacent to the glass-covered Galleria Mazzini, is Genoa's designer shopping street. It links Piazza Corvetto with Piazza de Ferrari. The old city's lanes are full of all kinds of traditional shops and vintage boutiques.

Via Garibaldi 12
HOMEWARES, DESIGN

(☑010 253 03 65; www.viagaribaldi12.com; Via Garibaldi 12; ⊙10am-2pm & 3.30-7pm Tue-Sat) Even if you're not in the market for designer homewares, it's worth trotting up the noble stairs here just to be reminded how splendid a city Genoa can be. There's an incredibly canny collection of contemporary furniture and objects on display, but it's the shop's original architecture – an aesthetic onslaught of columns, arched windows and baroque painted ceilings – that will make your jaw drop.

Butteghetta Magica di Tinello Daniela
HOMEWARES, NATIVITY SCENES

(☑010 247 42 25; Via della Maddalena 2; ⊙3-7pm Mon, 10am-1pm & 3-7pm Tue-Sat) Stock your kitchen from a selection of brightly glazed traditional ceramics and beautiful contemporary kitchenware. This is also the place to buy a *corzetti*, a carved wooden stamp that is used to make a local pasta speciality of the same name. If you're here during the Christmas season, the *magica* of the title comes into play with spectacular nativity scenes.

Pietro Romanengo fu Stefano
CHOCOLATES

See p22

❶ Information

Police Station (☑010 5 36 61; Via Armando Diaz 2)

San Martino Hospital (☑010 55 51; Largo Rosanna Benci 10)

Tourist Office (☑010 557 29 03; www.visit genoa.it; Via Garibaldi 12r; ⊙9am-5.30pm, to 8pm in summer)

❶ Getting Around

PUBLIC TRANSPORT

AMT operates buses throughout the city and there is an **AMT information office** (Via d'Annunzio 8; ⊙7.15am-6pm Mon-Fri, 7am-7pm Sat & Sun) at the bus terminal. Bus line 383 links Stazione Brignole with Piazza de Ferrari and Stazione Principe. A ticket valid for 90 minutes costs €1.50. Tickets can be used on main-line trains within the city limits, as well as on the **metro** (www.genovametro.com).

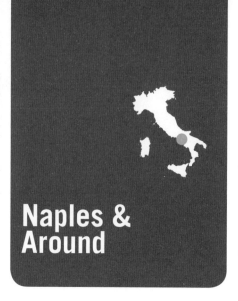

Italy's most misunderstood city is also one of its most intriguing – an exhilarating mess of bombastic baroque interiors, cocky baristas and subterranean ruins.

NAPLES

POP 989,110

According to legend, traders from Rhodes established the city on the island of Megaris in about 680 BC. Originally called Parthenope, it was eventually incorporated into a new city, Neapolis, founded by Greeks from Cumae in 474 BC. However, within 150 years it was in Roman hands, becoming something of a VIP resort favoured by emperors Pompey, Caesar and Tiberius.

After the fall of the Roman Empire, Naples passed through the hands of the Byzantines, the Normans, the German Swabians, the Angevins and the Spanish Bourbons. Aside from a Napoleonic interlude, the Bourbons remained until they were unseated by Garibaldi and the Kingdom of Italy in 1860. Naples was heavily bombed in WWII, and the effects can still be seen on many monuments around the city. Since the war, Campania's capital has continued to suffer. Endemic corruption and the re-emergence of the Camorra have plagued much of the city's postwar resurrection, reaching a nadir in the years following a severe earthquake in 1980.

Despite these tribulations, the winds of change are blowing. New ideas and innovation are driving a growing number of youth-run enterprises and businesses, while the city's famous art-themed metro launched another two starchitect-designed stations in 2015.

◉ Sights

Complesso Monumentale di Santa Chiara　　BASILICA, MONASTERY
(☑081 551 66 73; www.monasterodisantachiara. eu; Via Santa Chiara 49c; basilica free, Complesso Monumentale adult/reduced €6/4.50; ⊙basilica 7.30am-1pm & 4.30-8pm, Complesso Monumentale 9.30am-5.30pm Mon-Sat, 10am-2.30pm Sun; Ⓜ Dante) Vast and cleverly deceptive, the mighty **Basilica di Santa Chiara** stands at the heart of this tranquil monastery complex. The church was severely damaged in WWII: what you see today is a 20th-century recreation of Gagliardo Primario's 14th-century original. Adjoining it are the basilica's cloisters, adorned with brightly coloured 17th-century majolica tiles and frescoes.

Cappella Sansevero　　CHAPEL
(☑081 551 84 70; www.museosansevero. it; Via Francesco de Sanctis 19; adult/reduced €7/5; ⊙9.30am-6.30pm Mon & Wed-Sat, to 2pm Sun; Ⓜ Dante) It's in this Masonic-inspired baroque chapel that you'll find Giuseppe Sanmartino's incredible sculpture, *Cristo velato* (Veiled Christ), its marble veil so realistic that it's tempting to lift it and view Christ underneath. It's one of several artistic wonders that include Francesco Queirolo's sculpture *Disinganno* (Disillusion), Antonio Corradini's *Pudicizia* (Modesty) and colourful frescoes by Francesco Maria Russo, the latter untouched since their creation in 1749.

Duomo
CATHEDRAL

(☑081 44 90 65; Via Duomo 149; baptistry €1.50; ☺cathedral 8.30am-1.30pm & 2.30-8pm Mon-Sat, 8.30am-1.30pm & 4.30-7.30pm Sun, baptistry 8.30am-1pm Mon-Sat, 8.30am-12.30pm & 5-6.30pm Sun; 🚍C55 to Via Duomo) Whether you go for Giovanni Lanfranco's fresco in the Cappella di San Gennaro (Chapel of St Janarius), the 4th-century mosaics in the baptistry, or the thrice-annual miracle of San Gennaro, do not miss Naples' cathedral.

Museo Archeologico Nazionale
MUSEUM

See p28

Certosa e Museo
di San Martino
MONASTERY, MUSEUM

(☑081 229 45 68; www.polomusealenapoli.benicul turali.it; Largo San Martino 5; adult/reduced €6/3; ☺8.30am-7.30pm Thu-Tue; Ⓜ Vanvitelli, 🚍Montesanto to Morghen) The high point (quite literally) of the Neapolitan baroque, this charterhouse-turned-museum was founded as a Carthusian monastery in the 14th century. Centred on one of the most beautiful cloisters in Italy, it has been decorated, adorned and altered over the centuries by some of Italy's finest talent, most importantly Giovanni Antonio Dosio in the 16th century and baroque master Cosimo Fanzago a century later. Nowadays, it's a superb repository of Neapolitan artistry.

Palazzo Reale di Capodimonte
MUSEUM

(☑081 749 91 11; www.polomusealenapoli.beni culturali.it; Via Miano 2; adult/reduced €7.50/3.75; ☺8.30am-7.30pm Thu-Tue; 🚍R4, 178 to Via Capodimonte) Originally designed as a hunting lodge for Charles VII of Bourbon, this monumental palace was begun in 1738 and took more than a century to complete. It's now home to the Museo Nazionale di Capodimonte, southern Italy's largest and richest art gallery. Its vast collection – much of which Charles inherited from his mother,

Complesso Monumentale di Santa Chiara
PERSEOMEDUSA / SHUTTERSTOCK ©

Elisabetta Farnese – was moved here in 1759 and ranges from exquisite 12th-century altarpieces to works by Botticelli, Caravaggio, Titian and Andy Warhol.

☞ Tours

Tunnel Borbonico
HISTORIC SITE

(☑081 764 58 08, 366 2484151; www.tunnelbor bonico.info; Vico del Grottone 4; 75min standard tours adult/reduced €10/5; ☺standard tours 10am, noon, 3.30pm & 5.30pm Fri-Sun; 🚍R2 to Via San Carlo) Traverse five centuries along Naples' engrossing Bourbon Tunnel. Conceived by Ferdinand II in 1853 to link the Palazzo Reale to the barracks and the sea, the never-completed escape route is part of the 17th-century Carmignano Aqueduct system, itself incorporating 16th-century cisterns. An air-raid shelter and military hospital during WWII, this underground

---

❶ BEFORE YOU EXPLORE

If you're planning to blitz the sights, the Campania Artecard (☑800 60 06 01; www. campaniartecard.it) is an excellent investment. A cumulative ticket that covers museum admission and transport, it comes in various forms. The Naples three-day ticket (adult/ reduced €21/12) gives free admission to three participating sites, a 50% discount on others and free use of public transport in the city. Other handy options include a seven-day 'Tutta la Regione' ticket (€34), which offers free admission to five sites and discounted admission to others in areas as far afield as Caserta, Ravello (Amalfi Coast) and Paestum. The latter does not cover transport. Cards can be purchased online, at the dedicated Artecard booth inside the tourist office at Stazione Centrale, or at participating sites and museums.

Naples

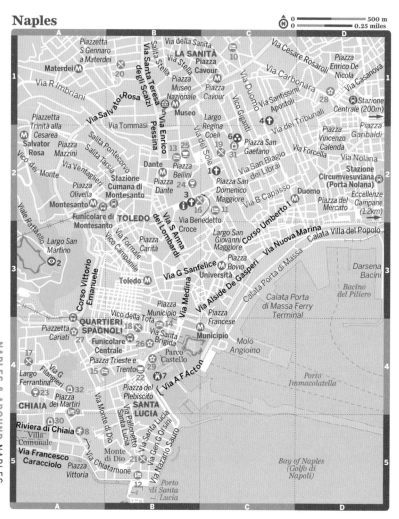

labyrinth rekindles the past with evocative wartime artefacts. The standard tour doesn't require prebooking, though the Adventure Tour (80 minutes; adult/reduced €15/10) and adults-only Speleo Tour (2½ hours; €30) do.

Napoli Sotterranea
ARCHAEOLOGICAL SITE

(Underground Naples; ☑ 081 29 69 44; www.napoli sotterranea.org; Piazza San Gaetano 68; adult/reduced €10/8; ⊙ English tours 10am, noon, 2pm, 4pm & 6pm; ☐ C55 to Via Duomo) This evocative guided tour leads you 40m below street level

to explore Naples' ancient labyrinth of aqueducts, passages and cisterns.

Kayak Napoli
KAYAKING

(☑ 331 9874271; www.kayaknapoli.com; tours €20-30; ☐ 140 to Via Posillipo) ✪ Popular tours along the Neapolitan coastline, gliding past often-inaccessible ruins, neoclassical villas and luscious gardens, as well as into secret sea grottoes. Tours cater to rookie and experienced paddlers, with day and night options. Meet at Via Posillipo 68 (Baia delle Rocce Verdi) in the Posillipo neighbourhood.

Naples

Tours subject to weather and should be booked ahead.

�֍ Festivals & Events

Festa di San Gennaro　　　　　RELIGIOUS
The faithful flock to the Duomo to witness the miraculous liquefaction of San Gennaro's blood on the Saturday before the first Sunday in May. Repeat performances take place on 19 September and 16 December.

Maggio dei Monumenti　　　　　CULTURAL
(⊙May) A month-long cultural feast, with concerts, performances, exhibitions, guided tours and other events across Naples.

Wine & The City　　　　　WINE
(www.wineandthecity.it; ⊙May) A two-week celebration of regional *vino*, with free wine tastings and cultural events in palaces, museums, boutiques and eateries throughout the city.

🛏 Sleeping

For maximum atmosphere, consider the *centro storico* (historic centre), where you'll have many of the city's sights on your doorstep.

Cerasiello B&B　　　　　B&B €
(☑338 9264453, 081 033 09 77; www.cerasiello.it; Via Supportico Lopez 20; s €40-60, d €55-80, tr €70-95, q €85-105; ⊠ 🖥; Ⓜ Piazza Cavour, Museo) This gorgeous B&B consists of four rooms with private bathroom, an enchanting communal terrace and an ethno-chic look melding Neapolitan art with North African furnishings. The stylish kitchen offers a fabulous view of the Certosa di San Martino, a view shared by all rooms (or their bathroom) except Fuoco (Fire), which looks out at a church cupola.

Nardones 48　　　　　APARTMENT €
(☑338 8818998; www.nardones48.it; Via Nardones 48; small apt €60-72, large apt €80-120; ⊠ 🖥; 🚍R2 to Via San Carlo) White-on-white Nardones 48 serves up seven smart mini-apartments in a historic Quartieri Spagnoli building. The five largest apartments, each with mezzanine bedroom, accommodate up to four; the two smallest, each with a sofa bed, accommodate up to two. Three apartments boast a panoramic terrace, and all have modern kitchenette, flat-screen TV and contemporary bathroom with spacious shower.

B&B Cappella Vecchia　　　　　B&B €
(☑081 240 51 17; www.cappellavecchia11.it; Vico Santa Maria a Cappella Vecchia 11; s €50-80, d €75-110, tr €90-140; ⊠ @ 🖥; 🚍C24 to Piazza dei Martiri) Run by a super-helpful young couple, this B&B is a first-rate choice in the smart, fashionable Chiaia district. Rooms are simple and upbeat, with funky bathrooms, vibrant colours, and Neapolitan themes. There's a spacious communal area for breakfast, and free internet available 24/7. Check the website for special offers.

CAMPI FLEGREI

Stretching west of Posillipo Hill to the Tyrrhenian Sea, the Campi Flegrei (Phlegraean, or 'Fiery', Fields) is home to some of Campania's most remarkable – and overlooked – Graeco-Roman ruins. Gateway to the area is the port town of Pozzuoli. Established by the Greeks around 530 BC, its most famous resident is the Anfiteatro Flavio (☑848 80 02 88; Via Nicola Terracciano 75; adult/reduced €4/2; ⊙9am-1hr before sunset Wed-Mon; ⓜPozzuoli, ⓡCumana to Pozzuoli), Italy's third-largest ancient Roman amphitheatre.

A further 6km west, Baia was once a glamorous Roman holiday resort frequented by sun-seeking emperors. Fragments of this opulence linger among the 1st-century ruins of the Parco Archeologico di Baia (☑081 868 75 92; www.coopculture.it; Via Sella di Baia; adult/reduced €4/2 Sat & Sun, Tue-Fri free; ⊙hours vary; ⓠEAV to Baia, ⓡCumana to Fusaro), its mosaics, stuccoed *balneum* (bathroom) and imposing Tempio di Mercurio once part of a sprawling palace and spa complex. While the ruins are free on weekdays, weekend visitors need to purchase their tickets at the fascinating Museo Archeologico dei Campi Flegrei (Archaeological Museum of the Campi Flegrei; ☑081 523 37 97; cir.campania. beniculturali.it/museoarcheologicocampiflegrei; Via Castello 39; admission Sat & Sun €4, Tue-Fri free; ⊙9am-2pm Tue-Sun, last entry 1pm; ⓠEAV to Baia), a further 2km south along the coast.

Yet another 2km south, in the sleepy town of Bacoli, lurks the magical Piscina Mirabilis (Marvellous Pool; ☑333 6853278; Via Piscina Mirabilis; donation appreciated; ⊙hours vary, closed Mon; ⓡCumana to Fusaro, then EAV bus to Bacoli), the world's largest Roman cistern. You'll need to call the custodian to access the site, but it's well worth the effort. Bathed in an eerie light and featuring 48 soaring pillars and a barrel-vaulted ceiling, the so-called 'Marvellous Pool' is more subterranean cathedral than giant water tank. While entrance is free, show your manners by offering the custodian a €2 or €3 tip.

Both the Ferrovia Cumana and Naples' metro line 2 serve Pozzuoli, and the town is also connected to Ischia and Procida by frequent car and passenger ferries. To reach Baia, take the Ferrovia Cumana train to Fusaro station, walk 150m north, turning right into Via Carlo Vanvitelli (which eventually becomes Via Bellavista). The ruins are 750m to the east. To reach Bacoli, catch a Bacoli-bound EAV Bus from Fusaro.

Unfortunately, the Campi Flegrei's second-rate infrastructure and unreliable public transport, plus the fickle opening times of its sites, make pretrip planning a good idea. Contact the tourist office (☑081 526 14 81; www.infocampiflegrei.it; Largo Matteotti 1a; ⊙9am-3pm Mon-Fri; ⓜPozzuoli, ⓡCumana to Pozzuoli) in Pozzuoli for updated information on the area's sights and opening times, or consider exploring the area with popular local tour outfit Yellow Sudmarine (p113).

Hotel Piazza Bellini
BOUTIQUE HOTEL €€

(☑081 45 17 32; www.hotelpiazzabellini.com; Via Santa Maria di Costantinopoli 101; d from €100; ❄@☎; ⓜDante) Only steps from buzzing Piazza Bellini, this sharp, contemporary hotel occupies a 16th-century *palazzo*, its mint white spaces spiked with original majolica tiles and the work of emerging artists. Rooms offer pared-back cool, with designer fittings, chic bathrooms and mirror frames drawn straight onto the wall. Rooms on the 5th and 6th floors have panoramic terraces.

Decumani Hotel de Charme
BOUTIQUE HOTEL €€

(☑081 551 81 88; www.decumani.it; Via San Giovanni Maggiore Pignatelli 15; s €99-124, d €99-164; ❄@☎; ⓜUniversità) This classic boutique hotel occupies the former *palazzo* of Cardinal Sisto Riario Sforza, the last bishop of the Bourbon kingdom. Simple, stylish rooms feature high ceilings, parquet floors, 19th-century furniture, and modern bathrooms with spacious showers. Deluxe rooms crank up *la dolce vita* with personal hot tubs. The *pièce de résistance*, however, is the property's breathtaking baroque salon.

La Ciliegina Lifestyle Hotel
BOUTIQUE HOTEL €€

(☑081 1971 8800; www.cilieginahotel.it; Via PE Imbriani 30; d €150-250, junior ste €200-350; ❄@☎; ⓜMunicipio) An easy walk from the hydrofoil terminal, this chic, contemporary slumber spot is a hit with fashion-

108

conscious urbanites. Spacious white rooms are splashed with blue and red accents, each with a top-of-the-range Hästens bed, flat-screen TV and marble-clad bathroom with water-jet Jacuzzi shower (one junior suite has a Jacuzzi tub).

Grand Hotel Vesuvio   HOTEL €€€
(☑081 764 00 44; www.vesuvio.it; Via Partenope 45; s/d €280/310; 🅿@🛜; 🚍128 to Via Santa Lucia) Known for hosting legends – past guests include Rita Hayworth and Humphrey Bogart – this five-star heavyweight is a decadent melange of dripping chandeliers, period antiques and opulent rooms. Count your lucky stars while drinking a martini at the rooftop restaurant.

 Eating

Pizzeria Gino Sorbillo   PIZZA €
(☑081 44 66 43; www.accademiadellapizza.it; Via dei Tribunali 32; pizzas from €3.30; ⏲noon-3.30pm & 7pm-1am Mon-Sat; 🅼Dante) Day in, day out, this cult-status pizzeria is besieged by hungry hordes. While debate may rage over whether Gino Sorbillo's pizzas are the best in town, there's no doubt that his giant, wood-fired discs – made using organic flour and tomatoes – will have you licking finger tips and whiskers. Head in super early or prepare to queue.

Pintauro   PASTRIES €
(☑348 7781645; Via Toledo 275; sfogliatelle €2; ⏲9am-8pm Mon-Sat, 9.30am-2pm Sun, closed mid-Jul–early Sep; 🚍R2 to Via San Carlo, 🅼Municipio) Of Neapolitan *dolci* (sweets), the cream of the crop is the *sfogliatella,* a shell of flaky pastry stuffed with creamy, scented ricotta. This local institution has been selling *sfogliatelle* since the early 1800s, when its founder supposedly brought them to Naples from their culinary birthplace on the Amalfi Coast.

Pizzeria Starita   PIZZA €
(☑081 557 36 82; Via Materdei 28; pizzas from €3.50; ⏲noon-4pm & 7pm-midnight Mon-Sat, 7pm-midnight Sun; 🅼Materdei) The giant fork and ladle hanging on the wall at this historic pizzeria were used by Sophia Loren in *L'Oro di Napoli,* and the kitchen made the *pizze fritte* sold by the actress in the film. While the 60-plus pizza varieties include a tasty *fiorilli e zucchine* (courgette, courgette flowers and *provola*), our allegiance remains to its classic *marinara.*

La Taverna di Santa Chiara   NEAPOLITAN €€
(☑339 8150346; Via Santa Chiara 6; meals €25; ⏲12.30-3pm & 7-11pm Wed-Mon; 🛜; 🅼Dante) Gragnano pasta, Agerola pork, Benevento *latte nobile:* this intimate, two-level eatery is healthily obsessed with small, local producers and Slow Food ingredients. The result is a beautiful, seasonal journey across Campania. For an inspiring overview, order the *antipasto misto* (mixed antipasto), then tuck into lesser-known classics like *zuppa di soffritto* (spicy meat stew) with a glass of smooth house *vino.*

Eccellenze Campane   NEAPOLITAN €€
(☑081 20 36 57; www.eccellenzecampane.it; Via Benedetto Brin 49; pizza from €6, meals €30; ⏲7am-11pm Sun-Fri, to midnight Sat; 🚍116, 192, 460, 472, 475) This is Naples' answer to Turin-based food emporium Eataly: an impressive, contemporary showcase for top-notch Campanian comestibles. The sprawling space is divided into various dining and shopping sections, offering everything from beautifully charred pizzas and light *fritture* (fried snacks) to finer-dining seafood, coveted Sal Da Riso pastries, craft beers and no shortage of take-home pantry treats. A must for gastronomes.

L'Ebbrezza di Noè   NEAPOLITAN €€
(☑081 40 01 04; www.lebbrezzadinoe.com; Vico Vetriera 9; meals €37; ⏲8.30pm-midnight Tue-Sun; 🅼Piazza Amedeo) A wine shop by day, 'Noah's Drunkenness' transforms into an intimate culinary hotspot by night. Slip inside for *vino* and conversation at the bar, or settle into one of the bottle-lined dining rooms for seductive, market-driven dishes like house special *paccheri fritti* (fried pasta stuffed with aubergine and served with fresh basil and a rich tomato sauce).

Ristorantino dell'Avvocato   NEAPOLITAN €€
(☑081 032 00 47; www.ilristorantinodellavvocato. it; Via Santa Lucia 115-117; meals €40; ⏲noon-3pm & 7.30-11pm, lunch only Mon & Sun; 🛜; 🚍128 to Via Santa Lucia) This elegant yet welcoming restaurant has quickly won the respect of Neapolitan gastronomes. Apple of their eye is affable lawyer turned head chef Raffaele Cardillo, whose passion for Campania's culinary heritage merges with a knack for subtle, refreshing twists – think gnocchi with fresh mussels, clams, crumbed pistachio, lemon, ginger and garlic.

🍷 Drinking & Nightlife

Caffè Gambrinus   CAFE
(☑ 081 41 75 82; www.grancaffegambrinus.com; Via Chiaia 12; ⊙ 7am-1am Sun-Thu, to 2am Fri, to 3am Sat; 🚉 R2 to Via San Carlo, Ⓜ Municipio) Grand, chandeliered Gambrinus is Naples' oldest and most venerable cafe. Oscar Wilde knocked back a few here and Mussolini had some of the rooms shut to keep out left-wing intellectuals. The prices may be steep, but the *aperitivo* nibbles are decent and sipping a *spritz* or a luscious *cioccolata calda* (hot chocolate) in its belle époque rooms is something worth savouring.

Spazio Nea   CAFE
(☑ 081 45 13 58; www.spazionea.it; Via Constantinopoli 53; ⊙ 9am-2am; 🛜; Ⓜ Dante) Aptly skirting bohemian Piazza Bellini, this whitewashed gallery features its own cafe-bar speckled with books, flowers, cultured crowds and al fresco seating at the bottom of a baroque staircase. Eye up exhibitions of contemporary Italian and foreign art, then kick back with a *caffè* or a Cynar *spritz*. Check Nea's Facebook page for upcoming readings, live music gigs or DJ sets.

Enoteca Belledonne   BAR
(☑ 081 40 31 62; www.enotecabelledonne.com; Vico Belledonne a Chiaia 18; ⊙ 10am-2pm & 4.30pm-2am Tue-Sat, 6.30pm-1am Mon & Sun; 🛜; 🚉 C24 to Riviera di Chiaia) Exposed-brick walls, ambient lighting and bottle-lined shelves set a cosy scene at Chiaia's best-loved wine bar – just look for the evening crowd spilling out onto the street. Swill, sniff and eavesdrop over a list of well-chosen, mostly Italian wines, including 30 by the glass. The decent grazing menu includes charcuterie and cheese (€16), *crostini* (from €6) and bruschettas (€7).

Galleria 19   CLUB
(www.galleria19.it; Via San Sebastiano 19; ⊙ 11pm-5am Tue-Sat; Ⓜ Dante) Set in a long, cavernous cellar scattered with chesterfields and industrial lamps, this popular *centro storico* club draws a uni crowd early in the week, and 20- and 30-somethings on Friday and Saturday. Tunes span electronica, commercial and house. Check the website for upcoming events.

☆ Entertainment

Options run the gamut from nail-biting football games to world-class opera. For cultural listings check www.incampania. it. Tickets for most cultural events are available from ticket agency **Box Office** (☑ 081 551 91 88; www.boxofficenapoli.it; Galleria Umberto I 17; ⊙ 9.30am-8pm Mon-Fri, 9.30am-1.30pm & 4.30-8pm Sat; 🚉 R2 to Piazza Trieste e Trento) or the box office inside bookshop **Feltrinelli** (☑ 081 032 23 62; www.azzurro service.net; Piazza dei Martiri 23; ⊙ 11am-2pm & 3-8pm Mon-Sat; 🚉 C24 to Piazza dei Martiri).

Teatro San Carlo   OPERA, BALLET
See p28

Centro di Musica Antica
Pietà de' Turchini   CLASSICAL MUSIC
(☑ 081 40 23 95; www.turchini.it; Via Santa Caterina da Siena 38; 🚉 funicular Centrale to Corso Vittorio Emanuele) Classical-music buffs are in for a treat at this beautiful deconsecrated church, an evocative setting for concerts of mostly 17th- to 19th-century Neapolitan works. Tickets usually cost €10 (reduced €7).

Lanificio 25   LIVE MUSIC
(www.lanificio25.it; Piazza Enrico De Nicola 46; admission €5-10; ⊙ 9pm-late Fri & Sat; Ⓜ Garibaldi) This Bourbon-era wool factory and 15th-century cloister is now a burgeoning party and culture hub, strung with coloured lights and awash with video projections. Live music (usually from 10pm) is the mainstay, with mostly Italian outfits playing indie, rock, world music, electronica and more to an easy, arty, cosmopolitan crowd.

🛍 Shopping

Tramontano   ACCESSORIES
(☑ 081 41 48 37; www.tramontano.it; Via Chiaia 143-144; ⊙ 10am-1.30pm & 4-8pm Mon-Sat; 🚉 C24 to Piazza dei Martiri) Tramontano has a solid rep for its exquisitely crafted Neapolitan leather goods, from glam handbags and preppy satchels to duffels and totes. Each year, a new bag, inspired by a classic song, whether it's Patti Smith's 'Kimberley' or Creedence Clearwater Revival's 'Proud Mary', is added to the Rock Ladies' Collection.

E. Marinella   FASHION
(☑ 081 764 42 14; www.marinellanapoli.it; Via Riviera di Chiaia 287; ⊙ 8am-8pm Mon-Sat, 9am-1pm Sun; 🚉 C25 to Riviera di Chiaia, C24 to Piazza dei Martiri) One-time favourite of Luchino Visconti and Aristotle Onassis, this vintage boutique is the place for prêt-à-porter and made-to-measure silk ties in striking patterns and hues. Match them with an irresistible selection of luxury accessories, including shoes, vintage colognes, and scarves for style queens.

La Scarabattola
CRAFTS

([☎] 081 29 17 35; www.lascarabattola.it; Via dei Tribunali 50; ⊕ 10.30am-2pm & 3.30-7.30pm Mon-Fri, 10am-6pm Sat; 🚇 C55 to Via Duomo) Not only do La Scarabattola's handmade sculptures of *magi* (wise men), devils and Neapolitan folk figures constitute Jerusalem's official Christmas crèche, the artisan studio's fans include fashion designer Stefano Gabbana and Spanish royalty. Figurines aside, sleek ceramic creations (think Pulcinella-inspired place-card holders) refresh Neapolitan folklore with contemporary style.

ℹ️ Information

Loreto-Mare Hospital (Ospedale Loreto-Mare; [☎] 081 254 27 01, emergency 081 254 27 43; Via A Vespucci 26; 🚌 154, 🚌 1, 2, 4) Central-city hospital with an emergency department.

Pharmacy (Stazione Centrale; ⊕ 7am-9pm Mon-Sat, to 8pm Sun) Inside the train station.

Police Station (Questura; [☎] 081 794 11 11; Via Medina 75; [M] Università) Has an office for foreigners. To report a stolen car, call [☎] 081 79 41 43.

TOURIST OFFICES

Head to the following tourist bureaux for information and a map of the city:

Tourist Information Office ([☎] 081 551 27 01; Piazza del Gesù Nuovo 7; ⊕ 9am-5pm Mon-Sat, to 1pm Sun; [M] Dante) Tourist office in the *centro storico*.

Tourist Information Office ([☎] 081 26 87 79; Stazione Centrale; ⊕ 8.30am-7.30pm; [M] Garibaldi) Tourist office inside Stazione Centrale (Central Station).

Tourist Information Office ([☎] 081 40 23 94; Via San Carlo 9; ⊕ 9am-5pm Mon-Sat, to 1pm Sun; 🚌 R2 to Via San Carlo, [M] Municipio) Tourist office at Galleria Umberto I, directly opposite Teatro San Carlo.

WEBSITES

In Campania (www.incampania.com) Campania's official tourist website.

Napoli Unplugged (www.napoliunplugged.com) Informative website covering sights, events, news and practicalities.

ℹ️ Getting There & Away

CAR & MOTORCYCLE

Naples is on the Autostrada del Sole, the A1 (north to Rome and Milan) and the A3 (south to Salerno and Reggio di Calabria). The A30 skirts Naples to the northeast, while the A16 heads across the Apennines to Bari.

On approaching the city, the motorways meet the Tangenziale di Napoli, a major ring road around the city. The ring road hugs the city's northern fringe, meeting the A1 for Rome in the east and continuing westwards towards the Campi Flegrei and Pozzuoli.

ℹ️ Getting Around

TO/FROM THE AIRPORT

Airport shuttle bus Alibus connects the airport to Piazza Garibaldi (Stazione Centrale) and Molo Beverello (€3 from selected tobacconists, €4 on board; 45 minutes; every 20 minutes).

Official taxi fares from the airport are as follows: €23 to a seafront hotel or to Mergellina hydrofoil terminal, €19 to Piazza Municipio or Molo Beverello ferry terminal, and €16 to Stazione Centrale.

BUS

In Naples, buses are operated by city transport company **ANM** ([☎] 800 639525; www.anm.it). There's no central bus station, but most buses pass through Piazza Garibaldi.

CAR & MOTORCYCLE

Vehicle theft, anarchic traffic and illegal parking 'attendants' make driving in Naples a bad option. Furthermore, much of the city centre is closed to nonresident traffic for much of the day.

ℹ️ TICKETS, PLEASE

If travelling on public transport in Naples and Campania, you will most likely be using TIC (Ticket Integrato Campania) tickets. Available from newspaper kiosks and *tabaccaio* (tobacconists), these integrated tickets are valid on bus, tram, funicular, metro and suburban train services in Naples, on regional Circumvesuviana and Cumana trains, and on EAV and SITA Sud buses across Campania. They are not valid on ferry and hydrofoil services. Ticket types and prices vary depending on where you want to travel.

The cheapest option is a *corsa semplice* (one-trip) ticket, valid for one trip within one travel zone only. The *biglietto orario* (multitrip ticket) allows for multiple trips within a specified time period and across any number of zones. Daily and multiday tickets are also available in some areas. Prices listed in this chapter are generally for *biglietto orario* tickets. Check the TIC website (www.tic-campania.net) for exact details.

East of the city centre, there's a 24-hour car park at Via Brin (€1.30 for the first four hours, €7.20 for 24 hours).

FUNICULAR

Three services connect central Naples to Vomero, while a fourth connects Mergellina to Posillipo.

METRO

Line 1 Runs from Garibaldi (Stazione Centrale) to Vomero and the northern suburbs via the city centre. Useful stops include: Duomo and Università (southern edge of the *centro storico*), Municipio (hydrofoil and ferry terminals), Toledo (Via Toledo and Quartieri Spagnoli), Dante (western edge of the *centro storico*) and Museo Archaeologica Nazionale.

Line 2 Runs from Gianturco to Garibaldi (Stazione Centrale) and on to Pozzuoli. Useful stops include: Piazza Cavour (La Sanità and northern edge of *centro storico*), Piazza Amedeo (Chiaia) and Mergellina (Mergellina ferry terminal). Change between lines 1 and 2 at Garibaldi or Piazza Cavour (known as Museo on Line 1).

Line 6 A light-rail service running between Mergellina and Mostra.

TAXI

Official taxis are white and have meters; always ensure the meter is running. There are taxi stands at most of the city's main piazzas or you can call one of the following taxi cooperatives. See the taxi company websites for a comprehensive list of fares.

Consortaxi (☏ 081 22 22; www.consortaxi. com)

Consorzio Taxi Napoli (☏ 081 88 88; www. consorziotaxinapoli.it)

Radio Taxi Napoli (☏ 081 556 44 44; www. radiotaxinapoli.it)

MT VESUVIUS & POMPEII

Looming over the Bay of Naples, stratovolcano **Mt Vesuvius** (☏ 081 239 56 53; adult/reduced €10/8; ☉ 9am-6pm Jul & Aug, to 5pm Apr-Jun & Sep, to 4pm Mar & Oct, to 3pm Nov-Feb, ticket office closes 1hr before the crater) has blown its top more than 30 times. Its violent outburst in AD 79 not only drowned Pompeii in pumice and pushed the coastline back several kilometres; it also destroyed much of the mountain top, creating a huge caldera and two new peaks. The most destructive explosion after that of AD 79 was in 1631, while the most recent was in 1944.

Each year about 2.5 million people pour in to wander the eerie shell of ancient Pompeii, a once thriving commercial centre. Not only an evocative glimpse into Roman life, the ruins provide a stark reminder of the malign forces that lie deep inside Mt Vesuvius.

Vesuvius itself is the focal point of the **Parco Nazionale del Vesuvio** (Vesuvius National Park; www.epnv.it), which offers nine nature walks around the volcano. A simple map of the trails can be downloaded from the park's website. Alternatively, **Naples Trips & Tours** (☏ 349 7155270; www. naplestripsandtours.com; guided tours €50)

Temple of Apollo, Pompeii

runs a daily horse-riding tour of the park (weather permitting). Running for three to four hours, the tour includes transfers to/from Naples or Ercolano-Scavi Circumvesuviana station, helmet, saddle, guide and (most importantly) coffee.

Note that when weather conditions are bad the summit path is shut and bus departures are suspended.

Sights

Ruins of Pompeii ARCHAEOLOGICAL SITE
(☑ 081 857 53 47; www.pompeiisites.org; entrances at Porta Marina, Piazza Esedra & Piazza Anfiteatro; adult/reduced €11/5.50; ⊗ 8.30am-7.30pm summer, to 5pm winter) The ghostly ruins of ancient Pompeii (Pompei in Italian) make for one of the world's most engrossing archaeological experiences. Much of the site's value lies in the fact that the town wasn't simply blown away by Vesuvius in AD 79 but buried under a layer of lapilli (burning fragments of pumice stone). The result is a remarkably well-preserved slice of ancient life, where visitors can walk down Roman streets and snoop around millennia-old houses, temples, shops, cafes, amphitheatres, and even a brothel.

Villa dei Misteri ARCHAEOLOGICAL SITE
This recently restored, 90-room villa is one of the most complete structures left standing in Pompeii. The Dionysiac frieze, the most important fresco still on-site, spans the walls of the large dining room. One of the biggest and most arresting paintings from the ancient world, it depicts the initiation of a bride-to-be into the cult of Dionysus, the Greek god of wine.

Follow Via Consolare out of the town through **Porta Ercolano**. Continue past **Villa di Diomede**, turn right, and you'll come to Villa dei Misteri.

Sleeping & Eating

The ruins are best visited on a day trip from Naples, Sorrento or Salerno; once the excavations close for the day, the area around the site becomes decidedly seedy. Most of the restaurants near the ruins are characterless affairs set up for feeding busloads of tourists. Down in the modern town are a few decent restaurants serving excellent local food.

ⓘ TOURS

You'll almost certainly be approached by a guide outside the *scavi* (excavations) ticket office: note that authorised guides wear identification tags. If considering a guided tour of the ruins, reputable tour operators include **Yellow Sudmarine** (☑ 329 1010328, 334 1047036; www.yellowsudmarine.com; 2hr Pompeii guided tour €110) and **Walks of Italy** (www.walksofitaly.com; 2½hr Pompeii guided tour €52), both of which also offer excursions to other areas of Campania.

If you'd rather eat at the ruins, the on-site cafeteria peddles the standard choice of *panini*, pizza slices, salads, hot meals and gelato.

President CAMPANIAN €€
(☑ 081 850 72 45; www.ristorantepresident.it; Piazza Schettini 12; meals €35; ⊗ noon-4pm & 7pm-midnight, closed Mon Oct-Apr; ☑ FS to Pompei, ☑ Circumvesuviana to Pompei Scavi-Villa dei Misteri) With its dripping chandeliers and gracious service, the Michelin-starred President feels like a private dining room in an Audrey Hepburn film. At the helm is charming owner-chef Paolo Gramaglia, whose passion for local produce, history and culinary creativity translates into bread made to ancient Roman recipes, slow-cooked snapper paired with tomato puree and sweet-onion gelato, and deconstructed *pastiera* (sweet Neapolitan tart).

ⓘ Information

Tourist Office (☑ 081 850 72 55; Via Sacra 1; ⊗ 8.30am-3.30pm Mon-Fri) Located in the centre of the modern town.

ⓘ Getting There & Away

Busvia del Vesuvio shuttle buses to Vesuvius depart from outside the Pompei-Scavi-Villa dei Misteri train station.

To get here by car, take the A3 from Naples. Use the Pompeii exit and follow signs to Pompeii Scavi. Car parks (approximately €5 per hour) are clearly marked and vigorously touted.

ROAD TRIP ESSENTIALS

Italy
Driving Guide

Italy's stunning natural scenery, comprehensive road network and passion for cars makes it a wonderful road-trip destination.

Driving Fast Facts

Right or left? Drive on the right

Manual or automatic? Mostly manual

Legal driving age 18

Top speed limit 130km/h to 150km/h (on autostradas)

Signature car Flaming red Ferrari or Fiat 500

INSURANCE

➡ Third-party liability insurance is mandatory for all vehicles in Italy, including cars brought in from abroad.

➡ If driving an EU-registered vehicle, your home country insurance is sufficient. Ask your insurer for a European Accident Statement (EAS) form, which can simplify matters in the event of an accident.

➡ Hire agencies provide the minimum legal insurance; you can supplement it if you choose.

DRIVING LICENCE & DOCUMENTS

When driving in Italy you are required to carry with you:

➡ The vehicle registration document

➡ Your driving licence

➡ Proof of third-party liability insurance

Driving Licence

➡ All EU member states' driving licences are fully recognised throughout Europe.

➡ Travellers from other countries should obtain an International Driving Permit (IDP) through their national automobile association. This should be carried with your licence; it is not a substitute for it.

➡ No licence is needed to ride a scooter under 50cc. To ride a motorcycle or scooter up to 125cc, you'll need a licence (a car licence will do). For motorcycles over 125cc you need a motorcycle licence.

HIRING A CAR

Car-hire agencies are widespread in Italy and prebooking on the internet is often cheaper. Considerations before renting:

➡ Bear in mind that a car is generally more hassle than it's worth in cities, so only hire one for the time you'll be on the open road.

➡ Consider vehicle size carefully. High fuel prices, extremely narrow streets and tight parking conditions mean that smaller is often better.

➡ Road signs can be iffy in remote areas, so consider booking and paying for satnav.

Standard regulations:

➡ Many agencies have a minimum rental age of 25 and a maximum of 79. You can sometimes hire if you're over 21 but supplements will apply.

Local Expert: Driving Tips

A representative of the Automobile Club d'Italia (ACI) offers these pearls to ease your way on Italian roads:

➡ Pay particular attention to the weather. In summer when it gets very hot, always carry a bottle of water with you and have some fresh fruit to eat. Italy is a sunny country but, in winter, watch out for ice, snow and fog.

➡ On the extra-urban roads and autostradas, cars have to have their headlights on even during the day.

➡ Watch out for signs at the autostrada toll booths – the lanes marked 'Telepass' are for cars that pay through an automatic electronic system without stopping.

➡ Watch out in the cities – big and small – for the Limited Traffic Zones (ZTL) and pay parking. There is no universal system for indicating these or their hours.

➡ To rent you'll need a credit card, valid driving licence (with IDP if necessary) and passport or photo ID. Note that some companies require you to have your licence for at least a year.

➡ Hire cars come with the minimum legal insurance, which you can supplement by purchasing additional coverage.

➡ Check with your credit-card company to see if it offers a Collision Damage Waiver, which covers you for additional damage if you use that card to pay for the car.

The following are among the most competitive multinational and Italian car-hire agencies.

Avis (☑199 100133; www.avis.com)

Budget (☑800 4723325; www.budget.com)

Europcar (☑199 307030; www.europcar.com)

Hertz (☑199 112211; www.hertz.com)

Italy by Car (☑091 6393120; www.italyby car.it) Partners with Thrifty.

Maggiore (☑199 151120; www.maggiore.it) Partners with Alamo and National.

Motorcycles

Agencies throughout Italy rent motorbikes, ranging from small Vespas to larger touring bikes. Prices start at around €80/400 per day/week for a 650cc motorcycle.

BRINGING YOUR OWN VEHICLE

There are no major obstacles to driving your own vehicle into Italy. But you will have to adjust your car's headlights if it's a left-hand-drive UK model. You'll need to carry the following in the car:

➡ A warning triangle

➡ A fluorescent reflective vest to wear if you have to stop on a major road

➡ Snow chains if travelling in mountainous areas between 15 October and 15 April

BORDER CROSSINGS

Aside from the coast roads linking Italy with France and Slovenia, border crossings into Italy mostly involve tunnels through the Alps (open year-round) or mountain passes (seasonally closed or requiring snow chains). Every vehicle travelling across an international border should display a nationality plate of its country of registration. The list below outlines the major points of entry.

Austria From Innsbruck to Bolzano via A22/E45 (Brenner Pass); Villach to Tarvisio via A23/E55

France From Nice to Ventimiglia via A10/E80; Modane to Turin via A32/E70 (Fréjus Tunnel); Chamonix to Courmayeur via A5/E25 (Mont Blanc Tunnel)

Slovenia Sežana to Trieste via SR58/E70

Coins

Always try to keep some coins to hand. They come in very useful for parking meters.

Switzerland From Martigny to Aosta via SS27/E27 (Grand St Bernard Tunnel); Lugano to Como via A9/E35

MAPS

We recommend you purchase a good road map for your trip. The best driving maps are produced by the **Touring Club Italiano** (www.touringclub.com), Italy's largest map publisher. They are available at bookshops across Italy or online at the following:

Omni Resources (www.omnimap.com)
Stanfords (www.stanfords.co.uk)

ROADS & CONDITIONS

Italy's extensive road network covers the entire peninsula and with enough patience you'll be able to get just about anywhere. Road quality varies – the autostradas are generally excellent but smaller roads, particularly in rural areas, are not always great. Heavy rain can cause axle-busting potholes to form and road surfaces to crumble.

Traffic in and around the main cities is bad during morning and evening rush hours. Coastal roads get very busy on summer weekends. As a rule, traffic is quietest between 2pm and 4pm.

Road Categories

Autostradas Italy boasts an extensive network of autostradas, represented on road signs by a white 'A' followed by a number on a green background. The main north–south link is the Autostrada del Sole (the 'Motorway of the Sun'), which runs from Milan (Milano) to Reggio di Calabria. It's called the A1 from Milan to Rome (Roma), the A2 from Rome to Naples (Napoli), and the A3 from Naples to Reggio di Calabria. There are tolls on most motorways, payable by cash or credit card as you exit. To calculate the toll price for any given journey, use the route planner on www.autostrade.it.

Strade statali State highways; represented on maps by 'S' or 'SS'. Vary from four-lane highways to two-lane main roads. The latter can be extremely slow, especially in mountainous regions.

Strade regionali Regional highways connecting small villages. Coded 'SR' or 'R'.

Strade provinciali Provincial highways; coded 'SP' or 'P'.

Strade locali Often not even paved or mapped.

Along with their A or SS number, some Italian roads are labelled with an E number – for example, the A4 autostrada is also shown as the E64 on maps and signs. This E number refers to the road's designation on the Europe-wide E-road network. E routes, which often cross national boundaries, are generally made up of major national roads strung together. The E70, for example, traverses 10 countries and includes the Italian A4, A21 and A32 autostradas, as it runs from northern Spain to Georgia.

Limited Traffic Zones

Many town and city centres are off-limits to unauthorised traffic at certain times. If you drive past a sign with the wording *Zona a Traffico Limitato* you are entering

Road-Trip Websites

AUTOMOBILE ASSOCIATIONS
Automobile Club d'Italia (www.aci.it) Has a comprehensive online guide to motoring in Italy. Provides 24-hour roadside assistance.

CONDITIONS & TRAFFIC
Autostrade (www.autostrade.it) Route planner, weather forecasts and the traffic situation in real time. Also lists service stations, petrol prices and toll costs.

MAPS
Michelin (www.viamichelin.it) Online road-trip planner.

Tutto Città (www.tuttocitta.it) Good for detailed town and city maps.

Driving Problem-Buster

I can't speak Italian, will that be a problem? When at a petrol station you might have to ask the attendant for your fill-up. The thing to do here is ask for the amount you want, so *venti euro* for €20 or *pieno* for full. And always specify *benzina senza piombo* for unleaded petrol and *gasolio* for diesel. At autostrada toll booths, the amount you owe appears on a read-out by the booth.

What should I do if my car breaks down? Call the service number of your car-hire company. The Automobile Club d'Italia (ACI) provides a 24-hour roadside emergency service – call ☑803 116 from a landline or mobile with an Italian provider or ☑800 116800 from a foreign mobile phone. Foreigners do not have to join but instead pay a per-incident fee. Note that in the event of a breakdown, a warning triangle is compulsory, as is use of an approved yellow or orange safety vest if you leave your vehicle.

What if I have an accident? For minor accidents there's no need to call the police. Fill in an accident report – Constatazione Amichevole di Incidente (CAI; Agreed Motor Accident Statement) – through your car-hire firm or insurance company.

What should I do if I get stopped by the police? The police will want to see your passport (or photo ID), licence, car registration papers and proof of insurance.

What if I can't find anywhere to stay? Always book ahead in summer and popular holiday periods. Italy doesn't have chains of roadside motels so if it's getting late head to the nearest town and look for signs for an *albergo* (hotel).

Will I be able to find ATMs? Some autostrada service stations have ATMs (known as *bancomat* in Italian). Otherwise, they are widely available in towns and cities.

Will I need to pay tolls in advance? No. When you join an autostrada you have to pick up a ticket at the barrier. When you exit you pay based on the distance you've covered. Pay by cash or credit card. Avoid Telepass lanes at toll stations.

Are the road signs easy to read? Most signs are fairly obvious but it helps to know that town/city centres are indicated by the word *centro* and a kind of black-and-white bullseye sign; *divieto fermata* means 'no stopping'; and *tutte le direzione* means 'all directions', i.e access to major roads or intersections.

a Limited Traffic Zone (ZTL) and risk being caught on camera and fined. Being in a hire car will not exempt you from this rule.

If you think your hotel might be in a ZTL, contact them beforehand to ask about access arrangements.

ROAD RULES

➡ Drive on the right side of the road and overtake on the left. Unless otherwise indicated, give way to cars entering an intersection from a road on your right.

➡ Seatbelt use (front and rear) is required by law; violators are subject to an on-the-spot fine.

➡ In the event of a breakdown, a warning triangle is compulsory, as is use of an approved yellow or orange safety vest if you leave your vehicle. Recommended accessories include a first-aid kit, spare-bulb kit and fire extinguisher.

➡ Italy's blood-alcohol limit is 0.05%, and random breath tests take place. If you're involved in an accident while under the influence, the penalties can be severe.

➡ Headlights are compulsory day and night for all vehicles on autostradas and main roads.

➡ Helmets are required on all two-wheeled transport.

➡ Motorbikes can enter most restricted traffic areas in Italian cities.

➡ Speeding fines follow EU standards and are proportionate with the number of kilometres that you are caught driving over the speed limit, reaching up to €2000 with possible suspension of your driving licence. Speed limits are as follows:

Autostradas 130km/h to 150km/h
Other main highways 110km/h
Minor, nonurban roads 90km/h
Built-up areas 50km/h

Road Etiquette

➡ Italian drivers are fast, aggressive and skilful. Lane hopping and late braking are the norm and it's not uncommon to see cars tailgating at 130km/h. Don't expect cars to slow down for you or let you out. As soon as you see a gap, go for it. Italians expect the unexpected and react swiftly, but they're not used to ditherers, so be decisive.

➡ Flashing is common on the roads and has several meanings. If a car behind you flashes it means: 'Get out of the way' or 'Don't pull out, I'm not stopping'. But if an approaching car flashes you, it's warning you that there's a police check ahead.

➡ Use of the car horn is widespread. It might be a warning but it might equally be an expression of frustration at slow-moving traffic or celebration that the traffic light's turning green.

PARKING

➡ Parking is a major headache. Space is at a premium in towns and cities and Italy's traffic wardens are annoyingly efficient.

➡ Parking spaces outlined in blue are designated for paid parking – get a ticket from the nearest meter (coins only) or *tabaccaio* (tobacconist) and display it on your dashboard. Note, however, that charges often don't apply overnight, typically between 8pm and 8am.

➡ White or yellow lines almost always indicate that residential permits are needed.

Road Distances (km)

Note
Distances between Palermo and mainland towns do not take into account the ferry from Reggio di Calabria to Messina. Add an extra hour to your journey time to allow for this crossing.

	Bari	Bologna	Florence	Genoa	Milan	Naples	Palermo	Perugia	Reggio di Calabria	Rome	Siena	Trento	Trieste	Turin	Venice
Bologna	681														
Florence	784	106													
Genoa	996	285	268												
Milan	899	218	324	156											
Naples	322	640	534	758	858										
Palermo	734	1415	1345	1569	1633	811									
Perugia	612	270	164	432	488	408	1219								
Reggio di Calabria	490	1171	1101	1325	1389	567	272	816							
Rome	482	408	302	526	626	232	1043	170	664						
Siena	714	176	70	296	394	464	1275	103	867	232					
Trento	892	233	339	341	218	874	1626	459	1222	641	375				
Trieste	995	308	414	336	420	948	1689	543	1445	715	484	279			
Turin	1019	338	442	174	139	932	1743	545	1307	702	460	349	551		
Venice	806	269	265	387	284	899	799	394	1296	567	335	167	165	415	
Verona	808	141	247	282	164	781	1534	377	1139	549	293	97	250	295	120

Italy Playlist

Nessun Dorma Puccini

O sole mio Traditional

Tu vuoi fare l'americano Renato Carsone

Vieni via con me Paolo Conte

That's Amore Dean Martin

Four Seasons Vivaldi

➡ Traffic police generally turn a blind eye to motorcycles or scooters parked on footpaths.

FUEL

➡ You'll find filling stations all over, but smaller ones tend to close between about 1pm and 3.30pm and on Sunday afternoons.

➡ Many have *fai da te* (self-service) pumps that you can use any time. Simply insert a bank note into the payment machine and press the number of the pump you want.

➡ Italy's petrol prices are among the highest in Europe and vary from one service station *(benzinaio, stazione di servizio)* to another. When this book was researched, lead-free petrol *(benzina senza piombo)* averaged €1.93 per litre, with diesel *(gasolio)* averaging €1.81 per litre.

SAFETY

The main safety threat to motorists is theft. Hire cars and foreign vehicles are a target for robbers and although you're unlikely to have a problem, thefts do occur. As a general rule, always lock your car and never leave anything showing, particularly valuables, and certainly not overnight. If at all possible, avoid leaving luggage in an unattended car. It's a good idea to pay extra to leave your car in supervised car parks.

RADIO

RAI, Italy's state broadcaster, operates three national radio stations – Radio 1, 2 and 3 – offering news, current affairs, classical and commercial music, and endless phone-ins. Isoradio, another RAI station, provides regular news and traffic bulletins. There are also thousands of commercial radio stations, many broadcasting locally. Major ones include Radio Capital, good for modern hits; Radio Deejay, aimed at a younger audience; and Radio 24, which airs news and talk shows.

Italy
Travel Guide

GETTING THERE & AWAY

AIR

Italy's main international airports:

Rome Leonardo da Vinci (Fiumicino; www.adr.it) Italy's principal airport.

Rome Ciampino (www.adr.it) Hub for Ryanair flights to Rome (Roma).

Milan Malpensa (www.milanomalpensa1.eu, www.milanomalpensa2.eu) Main airport of Milan (Milano).

Milan Linate (www.milanolinate.eu) Milan's second airport.

Bergamo Orio al Serio (www.sacbo.it)

Turin (www.turin-airport.com)

Bologna Guglielmo Marconi (www.bologna-airport.it)

Pisa Galileo Galilei (www.pisa-airport.com) Main international airport for Tuscany.

Venice Marco Polo (www.veniceairport.it)

Naples Capodichino (www.gesac.it)

Bari Palese (www.aeroportidipuglia.it)

Catania Fontanarossa (www.aeroporto.catania.it) Sicily's busiest airport.

Palermo Falcone-Borsellino (www.gesap.it)

Cagliari Elmas (www.sogaer.it) Main gateway for Sardinia.

Car hire is available at all of these airports.

CAR & MOTORCYCLE

Driving into Italy is fairly straightforward – thanks to the Schengen Agreement, there are no customs checks when driving in from neighbours France, Switzerland, Austria and Slovenia.

Aside from the coast roads linking Italy with France and Slovenia, border crossings into Italy mostly involve tunnels through the Alps (open year-round) or mountain passes (seasonally closed or requiring snow chains). The list below outlines the major points of entry.

Austria From Innsbruck to Bolzano via A22/E45 (Brenner Pass); Villach to Tarvisio via A23/E55.

France From Nice to Ventimiglia via A10/E80; Modane to Turin (Torino) via A32/E70 (Fréjus Tunnel); Chamonix to Courmayeur via A5/E25 (Mont Blanc Tunnel).

Slovenia From Sežana to Trieste via SS58/E70.

Switzerland From Martigny to Aosta via SS27/E27 (Grand St Bernard Tunnel); Lugano to Como via A9/E35.

SEA

International car ferries sail to Italy from Albania, Croatia, Greece, Malta, Montenegro, Morocco, Slovenia, Spain and Tunisia. Some routes only operate in summer, when ticket prices rise. Prices for vehicles vary according to their size. Car hire is not always available at ports, so check beforehand on the nearest agency.

The website www.traghettionline.com (in Italian) details all of the ferry companies in the Mediterranean. The principal operators serving Italy:

Agoudimos Lines (www.agoudimos.it) Greece to Bari (11 to 16 hours) and Brindisi (seven to 14 hours).

Endeavor Lines (www.endeavor-lines.com) Greece to Brindisi (seven to 14 hours).

Grandi Navi Veloci (www.gnv.it) Barcelona to Genoa (18 hours).

Jadrolinija (www.jadrolinija.hr) Croatia to Ancona (from nine hours) and Bari (10 hours).

Practicalities

➡ **Smoking** Banned in all closed public spaces.

➡ **Time** Italy uses the 24-hour clock and is on Central European Time, one hour ahead of GMT/UTC.

➡ **TV & DVD** The main TV channels: state-run RAI-1, RAI-2 and RAI-3; Canale 5, Italia 1 and Rete 4; and La 7. Italian DVDs are regionally coded 2.

➡ **Weights & Measures** Italy uses the metric system, so kilometres not miles, litres not gallons.

Minoan Lines (www.minoan.gr) Greece to Venice (22 to 30 hours) and Ancona (16 to 22 hours).

Montenegro Lines (www.montenegrolines. net) Bar to Bari (nine hours).

Superfast (www.superfast.com) Greece to Bari (11 to 16 hours) and Ancona (16 to 22 hours).

Ventouris (www.ventouris.gr) Albania to Bari (eight hours).

TRAIN

Regular trains on two western lines connect Italy with France (one along the coast and the other from Turin into the French Alps). Trains from Milan head north into Switzerland and on towards the Benelux countries. Further east, two lines connect with Central and Eastern Europe.

Trenitalia (www.trenitalia.com) offers various train and car-hire packages that allow you to save on hire charges when you book a train ticket – see the website for details.

DIRECTORY A–Z

ACCOMMODATION

From dreamy villas to chic boutique hotels, historic hideaways and ravishing farmstays, Italy offers accommodation to suit every taste and budget.

Seasons & Rates

➡ Hotel rates fluctuate enormously from high to low season, and even from day to day depending on demand, season and booking method (online, through an agency etc).

➡ As a rule, peak rates apply at Easter, in summer and over the Christmas/New Year period. But there are exceptions – in the mountains, high season means the ski season (December to late March). Also, August is high season on the coast but low season in many cities where hotels offer discounts.

➡ Southern Italy is generally cheaper than the north.

Reservations

➡ Always book ahead in peak season, even if it's only for the first night or two.

➡ In the off-season, it always pays to call ahead to check that your hotel is open. Many coastal hotels close for winter, typically opening from late March to late October.

➡ Hotels usually require that reservations be confirmed with a credit-card number. No-shows will be docked a night's accommodation.

B&Bs

B&Bs can be found throughout the country in both urban and rural settings. Options include restored farmhouses, city *palazzi* (mansions), seaside bungalows and rooms in family houses. Prices vary but as a rule B&Bs are often better value than hotels in the same category. Note that breakfast in an Italian B&B will often be a continental combination of bread rolls, croissants, ham and cheese. For more information, contact **Bed & Breakfast Italia** (www.bbitalia.it).

Hotels & Pensioni

A *pensione* is a small, family-run hotel or guesthouse. Hotels are bigger and more expensive than *pensioni*, although at the cheaper end of the market, there's often little difference between the two. All hotels are rated from one to five stars, although this rating relates to facilities only and

---

Sleeping Price Ranges

The price ranges listed in this book refer to a double room with bathroom.

€ less than €110

€€ €110–€200

€€€ more than €200

gives no indication of value, comfort, atmosphere or friendliness.

Breakfast in cheaper hotels is rarely worth setting the alarm for. If you have the option, save your money and pop into a bar for a coffee and *cornetto* (croissant).

➡ One-star hotels and *pensioni* tend to be basic and often do not offer private bathrooms.

➡ Two-star places are similar but rooms will generally have a private bathroom.

➡ Three-star hotel rooms will come with a hairdryer, minibar (or fridge), safe and air-con. Many will also have satellite TV and wifi.

➡ Four- and five-star hotels offer facilities such as room service, laundry and dry-cleaning.

Agriturismi

From rustic country houses to luxurious estates and fully functioning farms, Italian farmstays, known as *agriturismi* (singular – *agriturismo*) are hugely popular. Comfort levels, facilities and prices vary accordingly but the best will offer swimming pools and top-class accommodation. Many also operate restaurants specialising in traditional local cuisine.

Agriturismi have long thrived in Tuscany and Umbria, but you'll now find them across the country. For listings and further details, check out the following sites:

Agriturismo.com (www.agriturismo.com)

Agriturismo.it (www.agriturismo.it)

Agriturismo-Italia.net (www.agriturismo-italia.net)

Agriturismo.net (www.agriturismo.net)

Agriturismo Vero (www.agriturismovero.com)

Agriturist (www.agriturist.com)

Other Options

Camping A popular summer option. Most campsites are big, summer-only complexes with swimming pools, restaurants and supermarkets. Many have space for RVs and offer bungalows or simple, self-contained flats. Minimum stays sometimes apply in high season. Check out www.campeggi.com and www.camping.it.

Hostels Hostels around the country offer dorm beds and private rooms. Breakfast is usually included in rates and dinner is sometimes available for about €10. For listings and further details, see www.aighostels.com or www.hostelworld.com.

Book Your Stay Online

For more accommodation reviews by Lonely Planet authors, check out http://hotels.lonelyplanet.com/italy. You'll find independent reviews, as well as recommendations on the best places to stay. Best of all, you can book online.

Convents & Monasteries Some convents and monasteries provide basic accommodation. Expect curfews, few frills and value for money. Useful resources include www.monasterystays.com, www.initaly.com/agri/convents.htm and www.santasusanna.org/comingToRome/convents.html.

Refuges Mountain huts kitted out with bunk rooms sleeping anything from two to a dozen or more people. Many offer half-board (bed, breakfast and dinner) and most are open from mid-June to mid-September.

Villas Villas and *fattorie* (farmhouses) can be rented in their entirety or sometimes by the room. Many have swimming pools.

ELECTRICITY

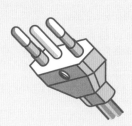

230V/50Hz

120V/60Hz

FOOD

A full Italian meal consists of an antipasto (appetiser), *primo* (first course, usually a pasta, risotto or polenta), *secondo* (second course, meat or fish) with *contorno* (vegetable side dish) or *insalata* (salad), and *dolce* (dessert) and/or fruit. When eating out it's perfectly OK to mix and match and order, say, a *primo* followed by an *insalata* or *contorno*.

Where to Eat

Trattorias Traditional, often family-run eateries offering simple, local food and wine. Some newer-wave trattorias offer more creative fare and scholarly wine lists. Generally cheap to midrange in price.

Eating Price Ranges

The following price ranges refer to a meal consisting of a *primo* (first course), *secondo* (second course), *dolce* (dessert) and a glass of house wine for one:

€ less than €25

€€ €25–€45

€€€ more than €45

Restaurants More formal, and more expensive, than trattorias, with more choice and smarter service. Reservations are generally required for popular and top-end places.

Pizzerias Alongside pizza, many pizzerias also offer antipasti, pastas, meat and vegetable dishes. They're often only open in the evening. The best have a wood-oven *(forno a legna)*.

Bars & Cafes Italians often breakfast on *cornetti* and coffee at a bar or cafe. Many bars and cafes sell *panini* (bread rolls with simple fillings) at lunchtime and serve a hot and cold buffet during the early evening *aperitivo* (aperitif) hour.

Wine Bars At an *enoteca* (plural – *enoteche*) you can drink wine by the glass and eat snacks such as cheeses, cold meats, bruschette and *crostini* (little toasts). Some also serve hot dishes.

Markets Most towns and cities have morning produce markets where you can stock up on picnic provisions. Villages might have a weekly market.

GAY & LESBIAN TRAVELLERS

➡ Homosexuality is legal in Italy and well tolerated in the major cities. However, overt displays of affection by homosexual couples could attract a negative response, particularly in the more conservative south and in smaller towns.

➡ There are gay clubs in Rome, Milan and Bologna, and a handful in places such as Florence. Some coastal towns and resorts (such as Viareggio in Tuscany and Taormina in Sicily) see much more action in summer.

Useful resources:

Arcigay & Arcilesbica (www.arcigay.it) Bologna-based national organisation for gays and lesbians.

GayFriendlyItaly.com (www.gayfriendly italy.com) English-language site produced by Gay.it, with information on everything from hotels to homophobia issues and the law.

Gay.it (www.gay.it) Website listing gay bars and hotels across the country.

Pride (www.prideonline.it) National monthly magazine of art, music, politics and gay culture.

HEALTH

➡ Italy has a public health system that is legally bound to provide emergency care to everyone.

➡ EU nationals are entitled to reduced-cost, sometimes free, medical care with a European Health Insurance Card (EHIC), available from your home health authority.

➡ Non-EU citizens should take out medical insurance.

➡ For emergency treatment, you can go to the *pronto soccorso* (casualty) section of an *ospedale* (public hospital), though be prepared for a long wait.

➡ Pharmacists can give advice and sell over-the-counter medication for minor illnesses. Pharmacies generally keep the same hours as other shops, closing at night and on Sundays. A handful remain open on a rotation basis *(farmacie di turno)* for emergency purposes. These are usually listed in newspapers. Closed pharmacies display a list of the nearest ones open.

➡ In major cities you are likely to find English-speaking doctors or a translator service available.

➡ Italian tap water is fine to drink.

➡ No vaccinations are required for travel to Italy.

INTERNET ACCESS

➡ An increasing number of hotels, B&Bs, hostels and even *agriturismi* offer free wifi. You'll also find it in many bars and cafes.

➡ The 🛜 icon used throughout this book indicates wifi is available.

➡ Rome and Bologna are among the cities that provide free wifi, although you'll have to register for the service at www.romawireless.com (Rome) and www.comune.bologna.it/wireless (Bologna) and have an Italian mobile phone number.

➡ Venice (Venezia) offers pay-for wifi packages online at www.veniceconnected.com.

➡ Internet access is not as widespread in rural and southern Italy as in urban and northern areas.

➡ Internet cafes are thin on the ground. Typical charges range from €2 to €6 per hour. They might require formal photo ID.

➡ Many top-end hotels charge upwards of €10 per day for access.

Italian Wine Classifications

Italian wines are classified according to strict quality-control standards and carry one of four denominations:

DOCG (Denominazione di Origine Controllata e Garantita) Italy's best wines; made in specific areas according to stringent production rules.

DOC (Denominazione di Origine Controllata) Quality wines produced in defined regional areas.

IGT (Indicazione geografica tipica) Wines typical of a certain region.

VdT (Vino da Tavola) Wines for everyday drinking; often served as house wine in trattorias.

MONEY

Italy uses the euro. Euro notes come in denominations of €500, €200, €100, €50, €20, €10 and €5; coins come in denominations of €2 and €1, and 50, 20, 10, five, two and one cents.

For the latest exchange rates, check out www.xe.com.

Admission Prices

➡ There are no hard and fast rules, but many state museums and galleries offer discounted admission to EU seniors and students.

➡ Typically, EU citizens under 18 and over 65 enter free and those aged between 18 and 24 pay a reduced rate.

➡ EU teachers might also qualify for concessions. In all cases you'll need photo ID to claim reduced entry.

ATMs

ATMs (known as *bancomat*) are widely available throughout Italy and are the best way to obtain local currency.

Credit Cards

➡ International credit and debit cards can be used in any ATM displaying the appropriate sign. Visa and MasterCard are among the most widely recognised, but others such as Cirrus and Maestro are also well covered.

Tipping Guide

Taxis Round the fare up to the nearest euro.

Restaurants Many locals don't tip waiters, but most visitors leave 10% if there's no service charge.

Cafes Leave a coin (as little as €0.10 is acceptable) if you drank your coffee at the counter, or 10% if you sat at a table.

Hotels Bellhops usually expect €1 to €2 per bag; it's not necessary to tip the concierge, cleaners or front-desk staff.

➡ Only some banks give cash advances over the counter, so you're better off using ATMs.

➡ Cards are good for paying in most hotels, restaurants, shops, supermarkets and toll booths. Some cheaper *pensioni*, trattorias and pizzerias only accept cash. Don't rely on credit cards at museums or galleries.

➡ Check any charges with your bank. Most banks now build a fee of around 2.75% into every foreign transaction. Also, ATM withdrawals can attract a further fee, usually around 1.5%.

➡ In an emergency, call to have your card blocked:

Amex (☎06 7290 0347 or your national call number)

Diners Club (☎800 393939)

MasterCard (☎800 870866)

Visa (☎800 819014)

Moneychangers

You can change money in banks, at post offices or at a *cambio* (exchange office). Post offices and banks tend to offer the best rates; exchange offices keep longer hours, but watch for high commissions and inferior rates.

OPENING HOURS

Banks 8.30am to 1.30pm and 2.45pm to 4.30pm Monday to Friday.

Bars & Cafes 7.30am to 8pm, sometimes until 1am or 2am.

Clubs 10pm to 4am.

Post Offices Main offices 8am to 7pm Monday to Friday, 8.30am to noon Saturday; branches 8am to 2pm weekdays, 8.30am to noon Saturday.

Restaurants Noon to 3pm and 7.30pm to 11pm; sometimes later in summer and in the south. Kitchens often shut an hour earlier than final closing time; most places close at least one day a week.

Shops 9am to 1pm and 3.30pm to 7.30pm (or 4pm to 8pm) weekdays. In larger cities, department stores and supermarkets typically open 9am to 7.30pm or 10am to 8pm Monday to Saturday, some also on Sunday.

PUBLIC HOLIDAYS

Individual towns have public holidays to celebrate the feasts of their patron saints. National public holidays:

Capodanno (New Year's Day) 1 January

Epifania (Epiphany) 6 January

Pasquetta (Easter Monday) March/April

Giorno della Liberazione (Liberation Day) 25 April

Festa del Lavoro (Labour Day) 1 May

Festa della Repubblica (Republic Day) 2 June

Festa dei Santi Pietro e Paolo (Feast of St Peter & St Paul) 29 June

Ferragosto (Feast of the Assumption) 15 August

Festa di Ognisanti (All Saints' Day) 1 November

Festa dell'Immacolata Concezione (Feast of the Immaculate Conception) 8 December

Natale (Christmas Day) 25 December

Festa di Santo Stefano (Boxing Day) 26 December

SAFE TRAVEL

Italy is a safe country but petty theft can be a problem. There's no need for paranoia but be aware that thieves and pickpockets operate in touristy areas, so watch out when exploring the sights in Rome, Florence, Venice, Naples etc.

Cars, particularly those with foreign number plates or rental-company stickers, provide rich pickings for thieves – see p401.

In case of theft or loss, report the incident to the police within 24 hours and ask for a statement. Some tips:

→ Keep essentials in a money belt but carry your day's spending money in a separate wallet.

→ Wear your bag/camera strap across your body and away from the road – thieves on mopeds can swipe a bag and be gone in seconds.

→ Never drape your bag over an empty chair at a street-side cafe or put it where you can't see it.

→ Always check your change to see you haven't been short changed.

TELEPHONE

Domestic Calls

→ Italian telephone area codes all begin with 0 and consist of up to four digits. Area codes are an integral part of all Italian phone numbers and must be dialled even when calling locally.

→ Mobile-phone numbers are nine or 10 digits and have a three-digit prefix starting with a 3.

→ Toll-free (free-phone) numbers are known as *numeri verdi* and usually start with 800.

→ Non-geographical numbers start with 840, 841, 848, 892, 899, 163, 166 or 199. Some six-digit national rate numbers are also in use (such as those for Alitalia, rail and postal information).

International Calls

→ To call Italy from abroad, call the international access number (☑011 in the USA, ☑00 from most other countries), Italy's country code (☑39) and then the area code of the location you want, including the leading 0.

→ The cheapest options for calling internationally are free or low-cost computer programs such as Skype, cut-rate call centres and international calling cards.

→ Cut-price call centres can be found in all of the main cities, and rates can be considerably lower than from Telecom payphones.

→ Another alternative is to use a direct-dialling service such as AT&T's USA Direct (access number ☑800 172444) or Telstra's Australia Direct (access number ☑800 172610), which allows you to make a reverse-charge (collect) call at home-country rates.

→ To make a reverse-charge international call from a public telephone, dial ☑170.

Mobile Phones (Cell Phones)

→ Italy uses GSM 900/1800, which is compatible with the rest of Europe and Australia but not with North American GSM 1900 or the totally different Japanese system.

→ Most smart phones are multiband, meaning that they are compatible with a variety of international networks. Check with your service provider to make sure it is compatible and beware of calls being routed internationally (very expensive for a 'local' call). In many cases you're better off buying an Italian phone or unlocking your phone for use with an Italian SIM card.

→ If you have a GSM multiband phone that you can unlock, it can cost as little as €10 to activate a prepaid SIM card in Italy. **TIM** (Telecom Italia Mobile; www.tim.it), **Wind** (www.wind. it) and **Vodafone** (www.vodafone.it) offer SIM cards and have retail outlets across Italy. You'll usually need your passport to open an account.

→ Once you're set up with a SIM card, you can easily purchase recharge cards (allowing you to top up your account with extra minutes) at tobacconists and news stands, as well as some bars, supermarkets and banks.

Payphones & Phonecards

→ You'll find payphones on the streets, in train stations and in Telecom offices. Most accept only *carte/schede telefoniche* (phonecards), although some accept credit cards.

→ Telecom offers a range of prepaid cards; for a full list, see www.telecomitalia.it/telefono/carte-telefoniche.

→ You can buy phonecards at post offices, tobacconists and news stands.

Important Numbers

Italy country code (☑39)

International access code (☑00)

Police (☑113)

Carabinieri (military police; ☑112)

Ambulance (☑118)

Fire (☑115)

Roadside assistance (☑803 116 from a landline or mobile with an Italian provider; ☑800 116800 from a foreign mobile phone)

TOILETS

➡ Public toilets are thin on the ground in Italy. You'll find them in autostrada service stations (generally free) and in main train stations (usually with a small fee of between €0.50 and €1).

➡ Often, the best thing is to nip into a cafe or bar, although you'll probably have to order a quick drink first.

➡ Keep some tissues to hand as loo paper is rare.

TOURIST INFORMATION

Practically every village, town and city in Italy has a tourist office of sorts. These operate under a variety of names: Azienda di Promozione Turistica (APT), Azienda Autonoma di Soggiorno e Turismo (AAST), Informazione e Assistenza ai Turisti (IAT) and Pro Loco. All deal directly with the public and most will respond to written and telephone requests for information.

Tourist offices can usually provide a city map, lists of hotels and information on the major sights. In larger towns and major tourist areas, English is usually spoken.

Main offices are generally open Monday to Friday; some also open on weekends, especially in urban areas and in peak summer season. Info booths (at train stations, for example) may keep slightly different hours.

Tourist Authorities

The **Italian National Tourist Office** (ENIT; www.enit.it) maintains international offices. See the website for contact details.

Regional tourist authorities are more concerned with planning, marketing and promotion than with offering a public information service. However, they offer useful websites, such as:

Emilia-Romagna (www.emiliaromagna turismo.it)

Lazio (www.ilmiolazio.it)

Piedmont (www.piemonteitalia.eu)

Tuscany (www.turismo.intoscana.it)

Umbria (www.regioneumbria.eu)

Veneto (www.veneto.to)

Other useful websites include www.italia.it and www.easy-italia.com.

TRAVELLERS WITH DISABILITIES

Italy is not an easy country for travellers with disabilities. Cobbled streets, blocked pavements and tiny lifts cause problems for wheelchair users. Not a lot has been done to make life easier for the deaf or blind, either.

A handful of cities publish general guides on accessibility, among them Bologna, Milan, Padua, Reggio Emilia, Turin, Venice and Verona. Contact the relevant tourist authorities for further information. Other helpful resources:

Handy Turismo (www.handyturismo.it) Information on Rome.

Milano per Tutti (www.milanopertutti.it) Covers Milan.

Lonely Planet's free Accessible Travel guide can be downloaded here: http://lptravel.to/AccessibleTravel.

Useful organisations:

Accessible Italy (www.accessibleitaly.com) Specialises in holiday services for travellers with disabilities. This is the best first port of call.

Consorzio Cooperative Integrate (www.coinsociale.it) This Rome-based organisation provides information on the capital (including transport and access) and is happy to share its contacts throughout Italy. Its **Presidio del Lazio** (www.presidiolazio.it) program seeks to improve access for tourists with disabilities.

Tourism for All (www.tourismforall.org.uk) This UK-based group has information on hotels with access for guests with disabilities, where to hire equipment and tour operators dealing with travellers with disabilities.

VISAS

➡ EU citizens do not need a visa for Italy.

➡ Residents of 28 non-EU countries, including Australia, Brazil, Canada, Israel, Japan, New Zealand and the USA, do not require visas for tourist visits of up to 90 days.

➡ Italy is one of the 15 signatories of the Schengen Convention. The standard tourist visa for a Schengen country is valid for 90 days. You must apply for it in your country of residence and you cannot apply for more than two in any 12-month period. They are not renewable within Italy.

➡ For full details of Italy's visa requirements check www.esteri.it/visti/home_eng.asp.

 # Language

Italian sounds can all be found in English. If you read our coloured pronunciation guides as if they were English, you'll be understood. Note that ai is pronounced as in 'aisle', ay as in 'say', ow as in 'how', dz as the 'ds' in 'lids', and that r is strong and rolled. If the consonant is written as a double letter, it's pronounced a little stronger, eg *sonno son*·no (sleep) versus *sono so*·no (I am). The stressed syllables are indicated with italics.

BASICS

Hello.	*Buongiorno.*	bwon·*jor*·no
Goodbye.	*Arrivederci.*	a·ree·ve·*der*·chee
Yes./No.	*Sì./No.*	see/no
Excuse me.	*Mi scusi.*	mee skoo·zee
Sorry.	*Mi dispiace.*	mee dees·*pya*·che
Please.	*Per favore.*	per fa·*vo*·re
Thank you.	*Grazie.*	*gra*·tsye

You're welcome.
Prego.   *pre*·go

Do you speak English?
Parli inglese?   *par*·lee een·*gle*·ze

I don't understand.
Non capisco.   non ka·*pee*·sko

How much is this?
Quanto costa questo?   *kwan*·to *kos*·ta *kwe*·sto

ACCOMMODATION

Do you have a room?
Avete una camera?   a·*ve*·te oo·na *ka*·me·ra

How much is it per night/person?
Quanto costa per   *kwan*·to *kos*·ta per
una notte/persona?   oo·na *no*·te/per·*so*·na

DIRECTIONS

Where's ...?
Dov'è ...?   do·*ve* ...

Can you show me (on the map)?
Può mostrarmi   pwo mos·*trar*·mee
(sulla pianta)?   (soo·la *pyan*·ta)

EATING & DRINKING

What would you recommend?
Cosa mi consiglia?   *ko*·za mee kon·*see*·lya

I'd like ..., please.
Vorrei ..., per favore. vo·*ray* ... per fa·*vo*·re

I don't eat (meat).
Non mangio (carne).   non *man*·jo (*kar*·ne)

Please bring the bill.
Mi porta il conto,   mee *por*·ta eel *kon*·to
per favore?   per fa·*vo*·re

EMERGENCIES

Help!
Aiuto!   a·*yoo*·to

I'm lost.
Mi sono perso/a. (m/f)   mee *so*·no *per*·so/a

I'm ill.
Mi sento male.   mee *sen*·to *ma*·le

Call the police!
Chiami la polizia!   *kya*·mee la po·lee·*tsee*·a

Call a doctor!
Chiami un medico!   *kya*·mee oon *me*·dee·ko

Want More?

For in-depth language information and handy phrases, check out Lonely Planet's *Italian Phrasebook*. You'll find it at **shop.lonelyplanet.com**, or you can buy Lonely Planet's iPhone phrasebooks at the Apple App Store.

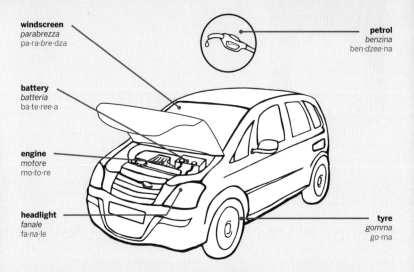

windscreen
parabrezza
pa·ra·bre·dza

petrol
benzina
ben·dzee·na

battery
batteria
ba·te·ree·a

engine
motore
mo·to·re

headlight
fanale
fa·na·le

tyre
gomma
go·ma

ON THE ROAD

I'd like to hire a/an ...	*Vorrei noleggiare ...*	vo·ray no·le·ja·re ...
4WD	*un fuoristrada*	oon fwo·ree·stra·da
automatic/ manual	*una macchina automatica/ manuale*	oo·na ma·kee·na ow·to·ma·tee·ka/ ma·noo·a·le
motorbike	*una moto*	oo·na mo·to

How much is it ...?	*Quanto costa ...?*	kwan·to kos·ta ...
daily	*al giorno*	al jor·no
weekly	*alla settimana*	a·la se·tee·ma·na

Does that include insurance?
E' compresa l'assicurazione?
e kom·pre·sa la·see·koo·ra·tsyo·ne

Signs

Alt	Stop
Dare la Precedenza	Give Way
Deviazione	Detour
Divieto di Accesso	No Entry
Entrata	Entrance
Pedaggio	Toll
Senso Unico	One Way
Uscita	Exit

Does that include mileage?
E' compreso il chilometraggio?
e kom·pre·so eel kee·lo·me·tra·jo

What's the city/country speed limit?
Qual'è il limite di velocità in città/campagna?
kwa·le eel lee·mee·te dee ve·lo·chee·ta een chee·ta/kam·pa·nya

Is this the road to (Venice)?
Questa strada porta a (Venezia)?
kwe·sta stra·da por·ta a (ve·ne·tsya)

(How long) Can I park here?
(Per quanto tempo) Posso parcheggiare qui?
(per kwan·to tem·po) po·so par·ke·ja·re kwee

Where's a service station?
Dov'è una stazione di servizio?
do·ve oo·na sta·tsyo·ne dee ser·vee·tsyo

Please fill it up.
Il pieno, per favore.
eel pye·no per fa·vo·re

I'd like (30) litres.
Vorrei (trenta) litri.
vo·ray (tren·ta) lee·tree

Please check the oil/water.
Può controllare l'olio/ l'acqua, per favore?
pwo kon·tro·la·re lo·lyo/ la·kwa per fa·vo·re

I need a mechanic.
Ho bisogno di un meccanico.
o bee·zo·nyo dee oon me·ka·nee·ko

The car/motorbike has broken down.
La macchina/moto si è guastata.
la ma·kee·na/mo·to see e gwas·ta·ta

I had an accident.
Ho avuto un incidente.
o a·voo·to oon een·chee·den·te

BEHIND THE SCENES

SEND US YOUR FEEDBACK

We love to hear from travellers – your comments help make our books better. We read every word, and we guarantee that your feedback goes straight to the authors. Visit **lonelyplanet. com/contact** to submit your updates and suggestions.

Note: We may edit, reproduce and incorporate your comments in Lonely Planet products such as guidebooks, websites and digital products, so let us know if you don't want your comments reproduced or your name acknowledged. For a copy of our privacy policy visit lonelyplanet.com/privacy.

ACKNOWLEDGMENTS

Climate map data adapted from Peel MC, Finlayson BL & McMahon TA (2007) 'Updated World Map of the Köppen-Geiger Climate Classification', *Hydrology and Earth System Sciences*, 11, 163344.

Cover photographs

Front: On the road to Badia a Passignano, Stefano Amantini/4Corners ©

Back: Roman ruins in Rome, S.Borisov/ Shutterstock ©

THIS BOOK

This 1st edition of *Grand Tour of Italy Road Trips* was researched and written by Cristian Bonetto, Duncan Garwood, Paula Hardy, Donna Wheeler and Nicola Williams. This guidebook was produced by the following:

Destination Editor Anna Tyler

Product Editor Vicky Smith

Senior Cartographers Anthony Phelan, Valentina Kremenchutskaya

Book Designers Michael Buick, Katherine Marsh

Assisting Editors Imogen Bannister, Kate Mathews, Tracy Whitmey

Assisting Book Designer Kerrianne Jenkins

Cover Researcher Naomi Parker

Thanks to Joel Cotterell, Brendan Dempsey, Grace Dobell, Kirsten Rawlings, Angela Tinson, Tony Wheeler

OUR STORY

A beat-up old car, a few dollars in the pocket and a sense of adventure. In 1972 that's all Tony and Maureen Wheeler needed for the trip of a lifetime – across Europe and Asia overland to Australia. It took several months, and at the end – broke but inspired – they sat at their kitchen table writing and stapling together their first travel guide, *Across Asia on the Cheap*. Within a week they'd sold 1500 copies. Lonely Planet was born.

Today, Lonely Planet has offices in Franklin, London, Melbourne, Oakland, Beijing and Delhi, with more than 600 staff and writers. We share Tony's belief that 'a great guidebook should do three things: inform, educate and amuse'.

INDEX

OUR WRITERS

PAULA HARDY
From Lido beaches to annual Biennales and *spritz*-fuelled aperitivo bars, Paula has contributed to Lonely Planet's Italian guides for over 15 years, including *Venice & the Veneto, Pocket Milan, The Italian Lakes, Sicily, Sardinia* and *Puglia & Basilicata*. When she's not scooting around the *bel paese*, she writes for a variety of travel publications and websites. Currently she divides her time between London, Italy and Morocco, and tweets her finds @paula6hardy.

CRISTIAN BONETTO
Thanks to his Italo-Australian heritage, Cristian gets to experience the *bel paese* (beautiful country) as both a local and an outsider. His musings on Italian cuisine, culture and style have appeared in media across the globe and his contributions for Lonely Planet include more than 30 travel guide editions, including *Naples & the Amalfi Coast, Venice & the Veneto, Denmark, New York City* and *Singapore*. Follow Cristian on Twitter (@CristianBonetto) and Instagram (rexcat75).

DUNCAN GARWOOD
A Brit travel writer based in the Castelli Romani hills just outside Rome, Duncan has clocked up endless kilometres walking around the Italian capital and exploring the far-flung reaches of the surrounding Lazio region. He's co-author of the *Rome* city guide and has worked on the past six editions of the *Italy* guide as well as guides to Piedmont, Sicily, Sardinia, and Naples and the Amalfi Coast. He has also written on Italy for newspapers and magazines.

DONNA WHEELER
Italy's border regions are Donna Wheeler's dream assignment: Alps, the sea, complex histories, plus spectacular wine and food. Donna has lived in Turin's Quadrilatero Romano and Genoa's centro storico and been an Italian-by-marriage for almost two decades. A former commissioning editor and content strategist, she's written guidebooks to Italy, France, Tunisia, Algeria, Norway and Belgium and publishes on art, architecture, history and food for LonelyPlanet.com, BBC.com Travel, National Geographic *Traveler* and My Art Guides. She is also the creative director of travel magazine *She Came to Stay*.

NICOLA WILLIAMS
British writer Nicola Williams lives on the southern shore of Lake Geneva. Thankfully for her Italianate soul, it is an easy hop through the Mont Blanc Tunnel to Italy where she has spent years eating her way around and revelling in its extraordinary art, architecture, cuisine and landscape. Hunting Tuscan white truffles in October is an annual family ritual. Nicola has worked on numerous titles for Lonely Planet, including those covering Italy, Milan, Turin & Genoa, and Piedmont. She shares her travels on Twitter @Tripalong.

Published by Lonely Planet Publications Pty Ltd
ABN 36 005 607 983
1st edition – Jun 2016
ISBN 978 1 76034 052 0
© Lonely Planet 2016   Photographs © as indicated 2016
10 9 8 7 6 5 4 3 2 1
Printed in China